A PARENTS' GUIDE TO

Special Education

IN NEW YORK CITY AND
THE METROPOLITAN AREA

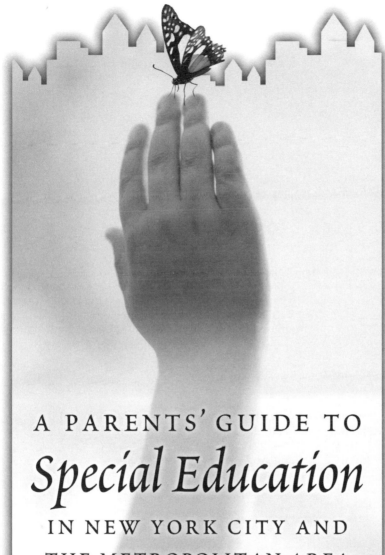

A PARENTS' GUIDE TO
Special Education
IN NEW YORK CITY AND
THE METROPOLITAN AREA

LAURIE DUBOS *and* JANA FROMER

Teachers College, Columbia University
New York and London

KH

Published by Teachers College Press, 1234 Amsterdam Avenue, New York, NY 10027

Library of Congress Cataloging-in-Publication Data

DuBos, Laurie.
    A parents' guide to special education in New York City and the
    Metropolitan area / Laurie DuBos and Jana Fromer.
        p.   cm.
    Includes bibliographic references and index.
    ISBN-13 978-0-8077-4685-1 (pbk : alk. paper)
    ISBN-10 0-8077-4685-1 (pbk : alk. paper)
    1. Special education—New York Metropolitan Area. 2. Private schools—
    New York Metropolitan Area—Directories. I. Fromer, Jana.

LC4033.N5D83 2006
371.909747'1—dc22   2006040418

ISBN-13: 978-0-8077-4685-1 (paper)
ISBN-10: 0-8077-4685-1 (paper)

Printed on acid-free paper

Manufactured in the United States of America

13   12   11   10   09   08   07   06   8   7   6   5   4   3   2   1

8/10/06

*To Hunter,
who brought us together*

Contents

PART III
SCHOOL PROFILES

PART IV
RESOURCES

Preface

There are many things that take parents by surprise, one of the earliest being the gut-wrenching feeling that first day when they bring their child to school. As parents you hope your child's teachers mirror the care and trust that you have in your child's school, that they are as considerate and caring as you need them to be. All parents want a school that provides the best education for their children. For parents with children with special needs, finding the appropriate school requires taking many paths, which can make for a difficult and prolonged journey.

Over the last 5 years we have had so many discussions concerning children and families with special needs that it began to feel like one very long conversation. At some point, we decided to stop talking and write this book. (Now, hopefully, we can start talking about something else!)

Our book is the product of the combination of our personal and professional experiences as a special education teacher and administrator and a mother familiar with the special education process. We visited as many schools for special education in New York City and its metropolitan area as we could, profiling each to include in this book.

At each school we encountered extraordinary people whose qualifications to teach children were supported by their humor, creativity, and compassion. You don't really learn how to be a special education teacher at graduate school; eventually the children teach you how they learn.

We created a parent survey—a form given exclusively to families whose children with special needs attended these private special education schools. Our purpose was to give parents the opportunity to share information regarding the programs they chose, the professionals they worked with, and the additional information they gathered along the way that has best served their child. The resources listed in Part IV of this book are based on the recommendations of parents who returned surveys to us. We are grateful to them for sharing this valuable information for the benefit of others.

We visited the schools listed with our notebooks and pencils, and little else to recommend us. We often left hours later, smiling, sometimes subdued, but always inspired. It's an understatement of extraordinary proportion to say that it's uplifting to meet good people who work on behalf of children. It's even better to write about them. We are grateful to the directors and staffs of the schools we visited, the experts we talked to, and the parents who took the time to share and examine their experiences with us, all of which have formed the heart of this book.

There were so many wonderful people who were instrumental to us during the process of writing this book. Our thanks to Brian Ellerbeck, our editor at Teachers College Press, for believing in the importance of this book and shepherding us through the process; to Susan Benson Gutentag, for smoothly and graciously editing us through our proposal; to Catherine Hausman, for her valuable advice and rock-solid support; and to Mary Ann Naples, our agent at The Creative Culture, Inc., for her extreme generosity and expertise. We would also like to thank Karen Beja, for giving us feedback on an earlier version of this book; Gabe Miller, for his fearless editing of our manuscript; and Na'ama Papadakos, for her hours of toil in checking resources. Thanks to Bill Dellinger for his painstaking ability to organize our lists and take our phone calls, even when they were about cooking.

Our huge love to a certain group of moms whose friendship we count on and treasure. They formed the path that led us to this book, and their continued support saw us through its completion.

Thanks to Clarence and Dottie DuBos, who supported and encouraged their daughter's education, and who have inspired her in so many ways.

Finally, thanks to Shirley Fromer, also known as Mom to Jana, for teaching her children and grandchildren the sweet and lasting effects of unconditional love by example. She knows the power of words and how to use them to effect change and illuminate lives. This is for her.

Introduction

Now, more than at any time in the past, a greater number of children in New York City are being identified as needing special education. As of 2005, there were 140,650 children identified as students with disabilities in New York City; over half of these students were enrolled in elementary and intermediate/middle schools (Hehir, Figueroa, Gamm, Katzman, Gruner, Karger, & Hernandez, 2005). Often, a large percentage of students with disabilities await placement for longer than the mandated 60 days, and many are not receiving the related services to which they are entitled.

Passed in 1975, Public Law 94–142 was the most comprehensive legislation passed by Congress to educate students with disabilities. Known as the Education for All Handicapped Children Act, this law assured a "free appropriate public education" for children aged 5 to 21 years, and laid the foundation for future legislation for children with disabilities. In 1990, the Individuals with Disabilities Education Act (IDEA) was passed, extending special education services from 3 to 5 years of age. IDEA was amended in 1997 to include early intervention programs for infants and toddlers with disabilities. These laws also created a mandate that expanded the roles of parents as equal partners in decisions relating to their children's education. As of 2004, IDEA was reauthorized as the Individuals with Disabilities Improvement Act, with changes to New York State law and regulations to become effective as of January 2006. As parents, you should educate yourselves about IDEA and its impact on your child's education. You have the right to participate throughout this process and are your child's strongest advocate.

Due to the high percentages of students not receiving special education services to which they are entitled in the public schools, there are an ever-increasing number of children coming from public and private independent schools seeking places in state-funded or private non-funded special education schools. While more children are being identified with learning and emotional difficulties (often after faltering in a mainstream setting), the number of available places in private special education schools is becoming increasingly scarce. Furthermore, those families whose children were diagnosed with special needs and received early intervention services are finding that the special education process changes as their child reaches the school-age years.

While some parents advocate for private school placement for their child, there are many parents who choose a public school placement for several reasons. First, their child may already be in a public school in their neighborhood, where the proximity to their home is important. This allows parents to become more involved in the school and the child to have friends nearby. This also means that parents do not have to consider transportation issues when their child attends a neighborhood public school. Second, the public school classroom may provide appropriate academic and social role models for their child. Many parents want their child to be in the least restrictive environment (LRE), which is required by law for children with special needs. Depending on the classroom profile, parents will often advocate for a public school placement, as they feel that their child's needs can best be served in the neighborhood school. Finally, there are financial reasons as to why many parents choose the public schools for their child. A public school placement is free, and parents do not have to undertake the possible costs of an attorney often required for placement in a private special education school.

HOW THIS BOOK IS ORGANIZED

In our attempt to provide you with as much detailed information as possible, we have organized this book into four parts. Part I (Chapters 1 through 5) is an overview of special education in New York City from kindergarten through grade 8. Part II (Chapters 6 through 9) describes the process of entering private special education schools in New York City. Part III contains profiles of 33 of these schools in New York City and the surrounding metropolitan area. Part IV lists resources—including doctors, therapists, hospitals, clinics, and agencies—that were provided by parents who have children in private special education schools, so that other parents could learn from their experiences. This information was gathered from surveys that were sent home to parents through the schools. In the four appendices, you will find a sample referral letter, a recommended checklist for school visits, a list of schools by classification, and a checklist for applications. Last but not least, as this field is filled with acronyms, we have provided a glossary at the end of the book which we hope will be helpful to you.

WHAT THIS BOOK WILL COVER

The information in this book is the culmination of our personal as well as our professional experiences. The list of private schools that are profiled in Part III of this book will assist parents in their search for a private school that best fits their child. Information is also included in Parts I and II to help parents with the transition from the Committee on Preschool Special Education (CPSE) to the Committee on Special Education (CSE). Additionally, in Part IV New York City educational resources created specifically for children with special needs are listed, as well as names of agencies and advocates who will work with you throughout this difficult process.

This book details specific recommendations and resources for parents and professionals in the New York City metropolitan area. Based on interviews with school directors and school tours, we have profiled 33 private schools in New York City and the surrounding metropolitan area that serve school-age children with special needs. The guide is intended to inform both you and the professionals with whom you work. We hope to help you arm yourselves with the skills and information necessary to navigate the special education system, from evaluation and classification to determining your child's eligibility for funding.

As of 2005, there were over 140,000 children classified for placement and/or related services in New York City (Hehir et al., 2005). Families looking for an appropriate placement for their child in a private nonpublic school are often overwhelmed and uninformed. Our desire is to provide you with information and confidence so that you may succeed in this process.

THE BASIC 5-STEP CHECKLIST

Following are the five basic steps that families with children with special needs must take. The accompanying stories are typical of families who at some point recognized that their child was responding differently. These parents were motivated to look for assistance that spoke more directly to their child's specific needs and development.

1. Identifying Your Child's Needs

Identifying a child's needs is an ongoing process for parents who at some point face the reality that their child is emotionally, physically, or developmentally delayed in a significant way. Children may begin to show these delays at different ages. A child below the age of 5 often first presents delays in speech, both expressive and receptive, which are sometimes accompanied by sensory integration issues.

There is no better judge of a child's progress than an observant parent. The realization that your child is developing differently may be immediately apparent, or it may be something you understand as time goes by. Early on, parents of children with special needs must recognize that they are the first to suspect that their child is not developing like their peers.

Lisa's Story

Lisa took her 4-year-old son to a local program that was billed as "Mommy, Music & Me!" Her son loved to listen to music at home. During the 6-week program, she spent every session chasing after her child when he refused to participate in circle time. It was a nightmare for her, and clearly not a fun activity for her child. It was only after completing the program that Lisa realized that while other children were at times unable to stay focused, her son was unable to participate each and every time. This was a wake-up call that resulted in her choosing a group activity more appropriate for her child. Her son was much more successful in a smaller group that lasted a shorter period of time and that didn't require as much interaction among the children.

2. Informing Yourself

Informing yourself is the next step. Initially, parents often contact professionals in medical fields or therapists. However, New York City has many other sources of information that are free and available to any parent in the five boroughs. You will find some of these listed in the resources in Part IV of this book.

Emma's Story

Emma was aware that her son was not very verbal, as he approached age 2½. Her pediatrician told her, "Boys typically are delayed in language." Meanwhile, her sister, a psychologist, urged her to take note of other behaviors. Was her child able to comprehend and respond to what people said to him? When Emma acted on this advice, she was able to determine that all communication, both expressive and receptive, was lacking or impaired in her child, and she was motivated to look for help.

3. Evaluating Your Child

Evaluating your child is best done as early as possible. Many families fear this initial process. There is an understandable desire to want to take a "wait-and-see" approach, hoping that your child develops without enlisting a team of experts. However, professionals agree that early intervention plays a significant and vital part in the treatment of a child's developmental needs and long-term progress. When your child is initially evaluated, not only does he or she begin to benefit immediately from the advice and recommendations of experts, your whole family does. A therapist might suggest various activities you can begin to do with your child at home, or various toys to buy to strengthen his/her motor skills. You might be advised to reexamine your living environment. It may be that putting away half the toys in the playroom will help your child to focus better while playing. We provide a list of tried and trusted professionals who are best equipped to evaluate your child, based on parent responses to our survey.

David's Story

David took his young daughter to the local playground every morning. He would bring her to the area designated for toddlers, and watch her interact with the other children of her age. While the other children were able to play comfortably within proximity of each other, his daughter never had an easy time. She would flinch and throw her arms out at the approach of any other child. Often she would hit a child who came too close to her. She would cry every time he brought her into the sandbox. The feel of sand against her skin appeared to actually hurt her. She was in perpetual motion across the playground without seeming to take in her surroundings. She appeared to need to expend a great deal of energy, while at the same time she resisted any interactions with others.

David knew that toddlers were not known for their ability to sit quietly and play with each other for a great length of time, but this was something entirely different. He brought his daughter to an evaluation center, which resulted in a recommendation to enroll her in a local Early Intervention program. There she received physical and occupational therapies 5 days a week. By attending along with her, David was able to observe and learn from the professionals as to how he could assist his daughter in better communicating and interacting with other children.

4. Entering the World of Special Education

Entering the world of special education is very stressful for most families. Finding a "label" that best describes and identifies your child can be an unwelcome and difficult experience. This is the point when families begin the process that separates them from the "typical" educational process. Instead of listing all of your child's abilities, you begin to categorize your child's disabilities. As agonizing as this is, it is done with the best of intentions, in order to get a school placement or the services your child needs.

You will be spending more time with your child's teachers and therapists than with your family and friends. You will begin amassing a small pile of paperwork that will eventually grow into multiple filing cabinets, filled with more reports on your child and family than you would ever have imagined possible. Eventually and unbelievably, you will find it tedious to talk and write about your child or rather, when doing so, prefer to highlight the strengths rather than list his or her challenges. This is a phenomenon unique to parents of children with special needs. Every parent would rather wax enthusiastic over their child's many extraordinary abilities (real or imagined!), but there is no place for indulgences on the form-filled road to special education. We think this is why these families form such tight and supportive bonds within the special education community.

Drawing from the personal, anecdotal experiences of the extensive special needs community, we are able to address the anxieties and concerns common to all parents but particularly relevant to those families who find themselves in the new, often unexpected, and frequently painful position of recognizing their children's delays, and who are coping successfully. These parents have the same high expectations and standards that all parents have for their children. Over time we have learned that the special needs community is a uniquely supportive one, with a boundless ability to interact and share information.

Amy's Story

Amy and her husband had their second child 5 years after their first son. It was immediately apparent to them that their youngest child (also a boy) was having trouble relating and responding easily when he was in the same situations that their older child had taken in stride.

Family reunions became a source of anxiety that began to outweigh the pleasure they had provided in the past. At age 5, their younger son was unable to cope with large gatherings of extended family. The high excitement often sent him into a tailspin, and often resulted in Amy having to remove her son from the rest of the family group. The disruption of his typical routine was unsettling to him, and he began to have behavior issues in his kindergarten class.

It was at the suggestion of his kindergarten teacher (an experienced professional who had seen similar issues occur with other children) that Amy and her husband took their son from the mainstream setting where he was faltering, and enrolled him in a program at a more appropriate school. His new kindergarten class was academically on a par with his last school, but the class size was significantly smaller, with more teacher support. The school offered occupational and physical therapies as well.

Within a short period of time, they saw tremendous improvement in their son's behavior and ability to succeed at school.

5. Locating a School

Locating a school is the final step. Our book lists private schools in New York City and the surrounding area for children with specific learning, language, and emotional or social difficulties. Private schools for special education come under two categories. One type is an independent private school, which is not funded by the New York City Department of Education (NYCDOE) and where parents are responsible for their child's tuition fees, but can seek all or partial reimbursement through due process. (We explain due process and other parent rights in Chapter 5 of this book.) The other type is known as a nonpublic school (NPS). This is a private school for special education that *is* funded through the NYCDOE.

Michael's Story

Michael's son had attended the local public school since kindergarten. The school was recognized as a high-achieving school where children scored well on the New York State reading and math tests. He had flourished well socially, and seemed to be keeping up academically. Michael and his wife lived and worked in the community and were very involved in their son's school events. However, their son began to demonstrate difficulties by 2nd grade. His reading comprehension and handwriting skills had always been below age expectations, but now the gap between his abilities and those of his peers was beginning to widen. His parents were advised to start afterschool tutoring, and they tried this, but it only resulted in more frustration for their child. At the recommendation of the tutor, they had their son evaluated privately. This evaluation revealed that their son had dyslexia as well as attention issues that impacted on his learning. Their evaluator was able to recommend several private schools that catered to children with learning disabilities similar to those of their son. They were fortunate enough to be offered a place at one of these schools. While this new school was not as conveniently located to their home, the difference it made for their child academically and emotionally within a year was well worth the change.

Our goal is to provide a practical handbook about special education in New York City and the metropolitan area for parents and professionals. We hope our efforts provide help and insight for those of you who are just beginning to navigate the world of special education as well as for those of you who have been a part of that world and have inspired us to write this book.

REFERENCE

Hehir, T., Figueroa, R., Gamm, S., Katzman, L. I., Gruner, A., Karger, J., & Hernandez, J. (2005). *Comprehensive management review and evaluation of special education.* Retrieved on March 22, 2006 from *http://www.nycenet. edu/NR/rdonlyres/0E84335C-D6B5-4B56-81AB-FDDE8EC61278/6227/ FinalHehirReport0920052.pdf*

PART I

Overview of Special Education in New York City

CHAPTER 1

What's So Special About Special Education?

Most children enter the public school system at kindergarten, where parents anticipate that their child will learn the skills that they will need during this first formal educational experience. For parents with children who stumble along the way, it becomes the beginning of identifying the resources and possible classroom settings that can support their learning. It is at this point that parents must undertake the role of advocate for their child in order to obtain the appropriate services and placement needed. While most parents are seeking a school where their child can learn alongside their typically developing peers in the public school system, many parents choose to consider the private and nonpublic schools available in New York City.

CHILDREN ENTERING KINDERGARTEN FROM THE COMMITTEE ON PRESCHOOL SPECIAL EDUCATION (CPSE)

Children who have been receiving preschool special education services through the Committee on Preschool Special Education (CPSE) are referred to the Regional Committee on Special Education (CSE), which opens each case to determine if a child continues to need special education services. To begin this process an evaluation must be completed, progress reports from current teachers and therapists will be requested, and an observation of the child in his/her current setting will be made. All of these will become a part of the child's case file. An Individualized Education Program (IEP) meeting will be held with the parents of children receiving CPSE services at the Regional CSE office to determine whether a child continues to need services, and an IEP will be written for those services to be provided, usually within a public school setting at the school-age level.

For parents whose child has been receiving preschool special education services and is entering kindergarten, there are several choices that may be considered within the continuum of services offered by the New York City Department of Education (NYCDOE). (The CSE will always consider the least restrictive environment where services can be provided within a regular classroom setting.) These are:

1. Declassification of support services
2. Supplementary aids and services
3. Special education teacher support services
4. Related services

Declassification of services means that a student no longer requires special education services; however, services are provided to the child or classroom teacher within the public school setting to assist with the transition to a regular classroom. Examples of support services are remediation and teaching and classroom modifications, as well as speech or counseling services.

Supplementary aids and services are meant to assist a child within the regular education classroom. These may include curriculum modifications, individualized assistance in the classroom, and behavior interventions. Services may be provided by related service personnel (i.e., speech therapist), a special education teacher, and/or a "para" (paraprofessional). A para is someone hired by the NYCDOE who assists the child during the school day (part-time or full-time) to support learning within the classroom. A child might also be assigned a paraprofessional to assist with health or management issues as part of the IEP.

Special education teacher support services are provided by a special education teacher. The special education teacher may work directly with your child or with your child's teacher toward adapting the classroom setting or in modifying teaching methods to assist your child while remaining in the regular education setting. This service can be provided for as little as 2 hours a week or as much as 50% of the school day.

Related services are any service that your child requires, such as speech/language therapy, occupational therapy, physical therapy, or counseling, as well as parent counseling/training, school health services (usually a nurse or paraprofessional), vision or orientation and mobility services, and hearing services. Related services may be the only special education service required by your child or it may be combined with other services, such as a special class or special education school. An IEP will identify the type of related service required for a child as well as the number of times/week (frequency), the length of time/session (duration), and the maximum group size (individualized or group) that the related service should be provided.

If a related service is recommended for a child and the NYCDOE is unable to provide a related service, parents can obtain a Related Service Authorization (RSA), which allows them to obtain a licensed independent provider of the service at no cost. The CSE can provide a list of independent providers to you, or you can find them at the Department of Education's Web site: *www.nycenet.edu/Parents/Essentials/Special+Education/documents.htm*

CHILDREN IDENTIFIED AFTER ENTERING PUBLIC SCHOOLS

For those children who are identified as having difficulties after starting their education in the public schools, the New York City public school system provides for the same continuum of services through the child's local public school, beginning with supplementary aids and services. As mentioned previously, these services begin by providing what are considered to be interventions that would allow a child to remain within the regular education classroom.

If a child requires more support or services, a referral is made for special education services. Based on evaluations and observations of the child, an IEP is developed that identifies those special education services that the child needs. At this point a child would be expected to remain in the regular education setting with special education teacher support services and/or related services such as those described earlier.

If a student continues to require more support after trying the services mentioned above, the next step on the continuum of services is called Collaborative Team Teaching (CTT). This service refers to a public school classroom in which there are two full-time teachers—a regular education teacher, and a special education teacher—and where children with disabilities are educated alongside their peers. The concept behind CTT is to provide the appropriate grade-level curriculum to all students while ensuring that instruction can be modified for those students who require such services. However, there have been a lot of kinks in getting the CTT concept to work.

Following CTT classrooms, special education services are delineated into special class services. These are identified according to the special class settings as follows:

1. Part-time placement in a regular education setting and part-time placement in a special class.
2. Full-time special class placement in a neighborhood public school.

3. Full-time special class placement in specialized schools within District 75, a citywide district for students with severe disabilities.
4. Full-time placement in a state-supported/operated school or New York State Education Department approved nonpublic school.
5. Placement in a home/hospital instruction setting.

At all times the NYCDOE is attempting to assure that your child is educated with typically developing children to the maximum extent possible within the least restrictive educational setting. The next step on the continuum of special education services would allow a child to spend part of the school day in a regular classroom and part of the day in a special class within the public school setting.

If your child requires more support, whether academic or behavioral, then a full-time special class placement in a neighborhood public school would be recommended. This is referred to as a self-contained special class in which students are supposed to be grouped with other children with disabilities who have similar academic, language, social, physical, and management needs. The student-to-teacher ratio varies depending upon the specific needs of the children placed in the classroom. This ratio is identified on page one of your child's IEP as the "staffing ratio." Staffing ratios for elementary grades can be 12:1 (12 students and 1 full-time special education teacher), 12:1:1 (12 students, 1 full-time special education teacher, and 1 full-time paraprofessional), 8:1:1 (8 students, 1 full-time special education teacher, and 1 full-time paraprofessional), or 6:1:1 (6 students, 1 full-time special education teacher, and 1 full-time paraprofessional). Those special classes having a higher teacher-to-student ratio (fewer students per teacher) are generally for those children who require more individualized support from adults and who are often characterized as needing intensive adult supervision and behavior management.

Another special class placement involves a staffing ratio of 12:1:4 (12 students, 1 full-time special education teacher, and 4 full-time paraprofessionals). These classes serve students who have multiple disabilities that would require a program in daily living skills, language and communication, and sensory stimulation, as well as therapeutic interventions.

Specialized public schools for students with severe disabilities (also referred to as District 75) provide programs for children classified as · deaf/hard of hearing or blind/visually impaired, as well as for children who are considered to be so severely disabled as to require intensive educational programming. District 75 schools are housed in schools that have only self-contained classes and can be found in certain New York City public schools. These are considered full-time placements for students and must be recommended by the CSE. Such a placement will limit the opportunities for a child to interact with typically developing peers; therefore, any opportunities with a child's peers must be identified in the child's IEP and must be supported by District 75 staff.

Next on the continuum of special education services available to students with disabilities are New York State-supported schools, of which there are several types.

- *State-Supported/Operated Schools* are schools that serve children classified as deaf, blind, severely emotionally disturbed, and/ or physically disabled who have been recommended by the CSE for placement in such a school. Some of these schools can provide residential care for children 5 days a week for those students who require intensive 24-hour programs during the school week.
- *Approved Nonpublic Day Schools (NPS-Day)* provide full-time self-contained classes for children with disabilities whose needs cannot be met within the New York City public school system. If an appropriate public school placement is not available or does not exist within the public school system, the CSE will refer a child to the Central Based Support Team (CBST). The CSE cannot make a recommendation for a specific nonpublic school; they must consult with the CBST in order to identify an appropriate nonpublic school. After a nonpublic school is identified and the child is accepted, then the CSE will reconvene to write the school's name on page one of the IEP under the Summary of Recommendations.
- *Approved Nonpublic Residential Schools (NPS-Residential)* are schools that provide 24-hour intensive educational programming within a highly structured residential setting. These schools are approved by the New York State Education Department (NYSED) and may be in New York or other states (such as New Jersey, Massachusetts, New Hampshire, and Pennsylvania). Again, the CSE must determine that there are no appropriate placements within the New York City public schools for a child to be considered for a residential setting and must consult with the CBST regarding such a placement. Obviously, such schools would be appropriate for those children who require 24-hour supervision and intervention.

- At the end of the continuum for special education services is *home and hospital instruction,* which includes educational services for children who are unable to attend school, usually due to illness or hospitalization, or due to emotional difficulties that prevent a child from attending school. A child could also be referred for home and hospital instruction if he/she is waiting for placement. At the elementary level at least 1 hour a day must be recommended. Home and hospital instruction must be recommended by the CSE and includes the following information on the child's IEP: number of hours, length of session, and number of times per week.

★   ★   ★

There are many possible placements within the public school system, as well as private schools available in New York City, to be considered by parents who are faced with the process of special education for their child. It is important to view each one in relation to your child's needs and to determine which placement would best meet your child's specific disabilities. You are embarking on a journey in unfamiliar waters, and familiarizing yourself with the choices available is the first step toward finding your way. Your child's best advocate is you, and you will benefit from as much knowledge and support as you can gather from the medical professionals, teachers, and therapists who work with or evaluate your child. Guiding your child through the process of placement in special education is truly a collaborative experience. There will be many outstanding individuals who will work effectively with you on behalf of your child—you will not be traveling alone.

CHAPTER 2

Referrals and Evaluations

A referral is the first step in working with the Committee on Special Education (CSE). It begins the process and a timeline in which the CSE must evaluate your child and, if your child is eligible, must arrange for special education programs and services. The timeline starts as soon as you given written consent for your child to be evaluated by the Department of Education. From that date the CSE has 60 days (school days, not including weekends or holidays) to evaluate your child and discuss the results of the evaluation with you, to develop the IEP, and to offer an appropriate placement. If your child is being recommended for placement in a state private school, the DOE must provide for these programs and services within 30 school days of the DOE receiving the recommendation from the CSE.

WHAT IS A REFERRAL AND WHO MAKES THEM?

A referral is essentially a letter that is forwarded to the local CSE, requesting that a child be evaluated to determine the need for special education services. Primary referral sources can be individuals such as parents, teachers, directors of preschool programs and day care centers, physicians, therapists, or social workers. Referrals can also be made through hospitals, public schools, public health facilities, social service agencies, other health care providers, and judicial officers. A sample referral letter can be found in Appendix A.

If your child is turning 5-years-old by December 31 (commonly called "turning 5" or "school age") and has been receiving special education services through CPSE, you should be contacted by the Committee on Special Education (CSE) in your region. This is to initiate an evaluation of your child to transition him/her into special education placement and services for kindergarten. You should contact the professionals who have been involved in your child's educational program and can provide current reports on your child's progress to assist you through the evaluation process.

Just because your child has been receiving services through CPSE does not mean that your child will be automatically approved for those services through CSE. Many parents are astonished to find out that there is little communication between these two entities, and that it can seem as though they are virtually starting over. Entering the special education process at kindergarten now means that you must consider public school programs for your child within the continuum of services available for children with disabilities. Since your child generally is expected to spend most of the school day in the classroom, he/she will receive fewer hours of services for speech, occupational, and physical therapies.

If your child has never received special education services and is being referred for an evaluation, he or she will receive an "initial evaluation." An initial evaluation requires your consent prior to any evaluation taking place. A parent may refuse to give consent for an evaluation, which generally results in closing a child's case. Closing a child's case means that your child will not be evaluated and, therefore, will not be eligible to receive services. It is important to note that the school or CSE may continue to pursue an evaluation of your child through mediation and due process procedures, as long as they follow New York state law regarding this. This is rarely done, but it is an available recourse to a public school or district.

It's always painful to hear that your child may not be developing comparatively to his/her peers. Parents are usually devastated when they are approached to have their child evaluated or, worse, to have their child asked to leave a program. If your child's school has contacted you regarding obtaining an evaluation for your child, it's best to work with the school to help you through this difficult process. If possible, have the director or principal write a letter as to why your child should be evaluated. You can include this along with your letter requesting an evaluation.

At that point you should become knowledgeable about the regulations and procedures that relate to New York state law pertaining to special education, evaluations, and the possible services that are available to your child. Much of this information can be obtained through the NYSED Web site, *www.nysed.gov.*

One of the considerations is whether you want to go through the CSE for an evaluation of your child free of cost, or if you want to consider an evaluation done by a private evaluator. If you choose to start with a private evaluation, you will be required to pay for it yourself. Occasionally, parents have part of the evaluation covered through their medical insurance; however, most insurance companies do not cover the cost of evaluations. Parents can obtain an independent educational evaluation (IEE), paid for by the NYCDOE, only if the parents disagree with the evaluation done by the CSE, and only if it can be proven that the NYCDOE evaluation is not appropriate. Parents still have the right to obtain their own evaluation at their own expense, which can be used as part of the IEP meeting and discussion.

If you choose to use the evaluation provided at public expense (meaning through the Board of Education), the CSE must give "notice" to you as the parent. Notice is usually given via a letter that describes the process for an evaluation as well as any possible tests that will be given to your child in order to obtain all relevant information regarding your child's current development. By law, no single test may be used as the sole basis for determining whether your child has a disability. All testing must be administered in your child's native language, must be reliable and valid for assessing your child's development, and must be administered by a trained and knowledgeable professional. Furthermore, any test must be nondiscriminatory and must assess a child in all areas of suspected disability. An observation in a child's current school setting is usually included as part of the evaluation.

WHAT DOES AN EVALUATION TELL YOU AND HOW DOES A PRIVATE SCHOOL USE IT?

An evaluation must include a physical examination, a psychological evaluation, a social history, and, depending on your child's age, educational tests or assessments. If your child is suspected of having a delay in other areas, such as speech or language, gross/fine motor, or emotional/behavioral development, further testing must be done to determine whether the delay is significant enough to warrant special education services. The results of these evaluations will identify whether your child is functioning at, above, or below age/grade-level expectations at the time of testing.

Private schools use evaluations to initially determine whether a child fits the profile of the school. While your child's entire evaluation will be considered, the test results (particularly IQ and academic skills), as well as the diagnosis assigned, are the primary indicators as to whether your child will be considered for placement. The schools will also review the recommendations at the end of the evaluation, as they usually include specific guidelines for a classroom setting, student–teacher ratio, related services, and teaching strategies.

WHAT TYPES OF EVALUATIONS ARE NEEDED
FOR APPLYING TO A PRIVATE SCHOOL?

Private special education schools often require specific types of testing for any child applying for admission. First, and foremost, schools want current evaluations. Current means within 1 year of your child's application to the school. Private special education schools want to know what your child's academic skills in reading, writing, and math are, as well as an assessment of his/her intellectual ability. As part of an evaluation, these schools are also interested in your child's ability to attend and focus in a classroom, his/her learning style, and whether your child requires highly individualized instruction (1:1) or can be educated in a small group setting. This information is usually based on the examiner's observations of your child throughout the testing or from an observation of your child in the classroom. Additionally, some reference is generally made in the evaluation about your child's emotional-social skills. This is often based on a discussion that the examiner has with the parents, as well as with a child's teacher and therapists.

In addition to educational and psychological testing, private schools want current reports from professionals who are working with your child—speech therapists, occupational therapists, physical therapists, psychologists, or social workers. In order to initiate or retain these related services for your child, reports must include testing information relevant to each field and recommendations as to whether therapy should be initiated, continued, or discontinued.

WHAT'S THE DIFFERENCE BETWEEN A PSYCHOEDUCATIONAL AND
A NEUROPSYCHOLOGICAL EVALUATION?

A private special education school will often specify whether a psychoeducational or a neuropsychological evaluation is required. A psychoeducational evaluation refers to a combination of psychological tests and educational assessments. This report, based on your child's test results, describes his/her strengths and weaknesses, gives appropriate recommendations for placement, and identifies strategies for assisting your child in an appropriate educational setting.

A neuropsychological evaluation includes both psychological and educational assessments as well as additional tests related to a child's executive functioning. Tests of executive functioning assess a child's skills in specific memory functioning, planning and organization, sustained attention, initiation, self-monitoring, fine motor skills, and/or behaviors. Most of these tests have questionnaires for a parent and a teacher to complete in order to identify a child's functioning across settings, particularly home versus school.

As mentioned earlier, parents can choose to pay for a private evaluation, although the NYCDOE will provide an evaluation of your child free of charge. The CSE in your region will schedule an evaluation, sometimes on a Saturday or after school, when your child is least likely to be at his or her best. The evaluation teams have limited time to spend with your child, as they are trying to accommodate several children within a specified time frame. We have heard from many parents that their child's evaluation was completed by the CSE in less than an hour. Thus, children's test results are often impacted by how comfortable they felt with an unfamiliar evaluator in an unfamiliar setting, and whether they could be adequately assessed in a very short period of time.

This does not mean that an evaluation by the NYCDOE is always inaccurate or of poor quality. As a parent it is important to know that you have to advocate for an evaluation that describes your child accurately. Remember, the CSE evaluators are testing thousands of children every year. They are required to assess your child using appropriate test instruments and will write their report based on these results. Therefore, parents who choose to use the NYCDOE to evaluate their child must be exceedingly mindful of what the report says about their child and, even more so, what it does not say about their child. If you feel that the evaluation does not reflect your child's current functioning in any area, you can request that an evaluation be done privately. Be prepared to argue your case with the team assigned to your child if necessary. Your child's teachers and therapists can be helpful at this point, since they work with your child on a daily basis and can attest to your child's abilities.

While costly, private evaluations are often preferred by parents, as they give a more detailed account of a child's learning difficulties. First, they are spread over several days in order to assess a child during optimal times, such as mornings. This means that a child will become more familiar with the evaluator and, hopefully, become more comfortable in the testing situation. By spending several days for testing, a private evaluator has more time to assess your child in areas that a CSE evaluator does not have the time to do. The result is a comprehensive report that includes specific details relative to your child's cognitive abilities, learning issues, language delays, and social-emotional development.

You will also need many copies of your child's current school reports, including classroom, related services, and any outside therapy reports, since most schools require these as part of your child's application packet. Since you are applying in the fall, this means that you would be sending reports from the previous year, as your child's school may not have a current report completed before the spring. If the school is unable to provide a current report, you can give permission to the director and your child's teachers and therapists to speak with the admissions director so that they can discuss your child's current skills and abilities, and any changes they've observed since the previous report.

While this seems like a formidable task, it is important that you keep focused on the timing involved for obtaining an appropriate placement for your child. Whether you are considering a public school or a private special education school for your child, having current reports and evaluations will help you move through this process more quickly so that you can consider all the available options.

CHAPTER 3

Eligibility Criteria

Eligibility for special education services is determined at an IEP meeting, after a team of professionals (including you) reviews your child's evaluations. Test results and other pertinent information regarding your child's current functioning and development are used to determine eligibility. Therefore, the results of any tests that are given to your child are an integral factor in determining whether your child meets the criteria for being classified as a student with a disability and, ultimately, the type of program and services your child will receive.

TESTING INFORMATION

Testing usually begins with a psychological evaluation and an educational assessment. For a psychological evaluation your child will most likely be assessed using the *Wechsler Intelligence Scale for Children* (Fourth Edition, 2003), or *WISC–IV*. If your child is very young (below 7 years), the psychologist may choose to use the *Wechsler Preschool and Primary Scale of Intelligence* (Revised Edition, 2002), or *WPPSI–R*. Most people refer to these tests as IQ tests, since they assess your child's expected intellectual capabilities. The *WISC–IV* identifies four index scores—Verbal Comprehension (VCI), Perceptual Reasoning (PRI), Working Memory (WMI), Processing Speed (PSI)—and a Full Scale IQ (FSIQ). The psychologist who evaluates your child can explain the test being used with him or her so that you understand how the scores are determined.

As part of evaluating your child, parents and teachers may also be asked to complete at least one rating scale that concerns a child's behaviors. These rating scales generally list statements describing children. You and the teacher are then asked to "rate" each statement as it pertains to your child. The rating may be answered in terms of frequency (i.e., never, sometimes, or often) or with a numerical scale such as 1 (never) to 5 (always). The scores on these tests are compared between home and school to identify specific areas of difficulty, such as your child's organizational skills or a possible attention deficit disorder.

Your child will be evaluated further by the psychologist to assess his/her skills in reading, math, written expression, general knowledge, and, for older students, science and social studies. Usually, the younger a child is, the fewer the number of tests given. This is due to the fact that younger children, who have not been exposed to the full range of academics, would not be expected to have attained skills above their age level (although some do). Also, younger children often have limited attention spans and have more difficulty in being tested over a longer period of time. For younger children, pre-academic skills are assessed in the areas of basic concepts (shapes, colors, letters, numbers) and fine motor skills (cutting skills, drawing basic shapes, etc.).

A child's reading abilities are usually assessed in at least three areas: sight words and decoding of words, comprehension (understanding what they read as well as what is read to them), and fluency (this includes the rate at which they are able to read and how fluid their reading is). Written expression includes spelling, grammar, punctuation, and other areas to determine your child's abilities in express himself/herself in writing. Testing will also be done on both math computation and word problems to determine if there are any deficits.

Occasionally, an educational evaluation will include some language tests, particularly if your child appears to have speech or language difficulties. These should not be confused with the testing done by a speech pathologist, who evaluates a child's speech and language skills to determine whether he or she exhibits a disorder or delay in either area. If your child is receiving services for speech, you should ask the speech therapist to coordinate testing with the evaluator so that the same tests are not being given to your child twice.

You should discuss the types of tests that your child will need for applying to schools with the evaluators you've chosen. They will be able to answer any specific questions that you may have and will discuss any additional testing that they feel would be appropriate for your child.

HOW TEST RESULTS IMPACT PROGRAMS AND SERVICES

Test results obtained from evaluations provide information that private schools use to determine whether a child would benefit from their program and services. At a minimum, schools want to know the functioning level of your child in several areas: intellectual abilities, academics, language, and social-emotional skills. The test results are used in the admissions process to determine whether your child is appropriate for the school and whether he or she fits the profile of a specific classroom.

Ultimately, the review of your child's entire evaluation will determine whether or not your child is asked to interview at the school.

CLASSIFICATIONS

One of the most difficult decisions that parents have to make is the classification of their child. Unlike the umbrella term "preschooler with a disability," the world changes when your child is turning 5. At this point in the special education process, all children are evaluated and classified according to specific criteria for each classification as determined by the New York State Education Department (NYSED). A student with a disability is defined as someone

> who has not attained the age of 21 prior to September 1st and who is entitled to attend public schools pursuant to section 3202 of the Education Law and who, because of mental, physical or emotional reasons, has been identified as having a disability and who requires special services and programs approved by the department. (Regulations of the Commissioner of Education, New York State Education Law, Section 4401, Part 200)

The criteria for determining a child's classification are listed in Table 3.1 so that you can review the basis by which children obtain special education services in New York City. The members of the Committee on Special Education (CSE) must use these criteria in determining your child's classification, based upon a review of your child's evaluation.

It is important to note that these classifications are educational classifications and not psychiatric or medical diagnoses. For instance, a child will not be classified as having a Pervasive Developmental Disorder (PDD) for the purposes of receiving services or placement in Special Education in New York City. PDD is not an educational classification; therefore, a child with a diagnosis of PDD would more likely be classified as either Speech Impaired (SI), Emotionally Disturbed (ED), or Autism (AUT). The classification of Speech Impaired would be given to a student diagnosed with PDD whose speech/language difficulties significantly impact his/her learning in a classroom. Emotionally Disturbed would be the classification given to a student diagnosed with PDD whose behaviors in social interaction and sensory regulation interfere with his/her learning in a classroom. At times, some students with this classification could also be described as emotionally fragile, withdrawn, or anxious.

Table 3.1. Classifications for Special Education Services

Classification	Definition and Criteria Required
Autism (AUT)	A developmental disability that significantly affects verbal and nonverbal communication and social interaction, which is generally evident before age 3, and which adversely affects a student's educational performance. Other characteristics often associated with Autism are: engagement in repetitive activities and stereotyped movements, resistance to environmental change or change in daily routines, and unusual responses to sensory experiences. A student who manifests the characteristics of Autism after age 3 could also be diagnosed as having Autism if the criteria in this paragraph are otherwise satisfied.
Deafness	A hearing impairment that is so severe that the student is impaired in processing linguistic information through hearing (with or without amplification) and that adversely affects a student's educational performance.
Deaf-blindness	Concomitant hearing and visual impairments, the combination of which causes such severe communication and other developmental and educational difficulties that a student cannot be accommodated in special education programs that are solely for students with deafness or students with blindness.
Emotional Disturbance (ED)	A condition in which a student exhibits one or more of the following characteristics *over a long period of time* and *to a marked degree* and that adversely affects the student's educational performance • an inability to learn that cannot be explained by intellectual, sensory, or health factors; • an inability to build or maintain satisfactory interpersonal relationships with peers and teachers; • inappropriate types of behavior or feelings under normal circumstances; • a generally pervasive mood of unhappiness or depression; or • a tendency to develop physical symptoms or fears associated with personal or school problems.
Hearing Impairment (HI)	An impairment in hearing, whether permanent or fluctuating, that adversely affects a student's educational performance but that is not included under the definition of deafness.
Learning Disability (LD)	A disorder in one or more of the basic psychological processes involved in understanding or in using language, spoken or written, which manifests itself in an imperfect ability to listen, think, speak, read, write, spell, or do mathematical calculations. This includes conditions such as perceptual disabilities, brain injury, minimal brain dysfunction, dyslexia, and developmental aphasia. It does not include learning problems that are primarily the result of visual, hearing, or motor disabilities, of mental retardation, of emotional disturbance, or of environmental, cultural, or economic disadvantage.

Mental Retardation (MR)	A disorder in which a student demonstrates significantly subaverage general intellectual functioning, which exists concurrently with deficits in adaptive behavior and manifested during the developmental period, and which adversely affects a student's educational performance.
Multiple Disabilities (MD)	Concomitant impairments (such as mental retardation/blindness, mental retardation/orthopedic impairment, etc.), the combination of which causes such severe educational needs that a student cannot be accommodated in a special education program solely for one of the impairments. It does not include deaf-blindness.
Orthopedic Impairment	A severe orthopedic impairment that adversely affects a student's educational performance. It includes impairments caused by congenital anomaly (e.g., clubfoot, absence of some member, etc.), impairments caused by disease (e.g., poliomyelitis, bone tuberculosis, etc.), and impairments from other causes (e.g., cerebral palsy, amputation, and fractures or burns that cause contractures).
Other Health Impairment (OHI)	An impairment that involves having limited strength, vitality, or alertness, including a heightened alertness to environmental stimuli, that results in limited alertness with respect to the educational environment, that is due to chronic or acute health problems, including but not limited to a heart condition, tuberculosis, rheumatic fever, nephritis, asthma, sickle cell anemia, hemophilia, epilepsy, lead poisoning, leukemia, diabetes, attention deficit disorder, attention deficit hyperactivity disorder, or Tourette's syndrome, which adversely affects a student's educational performance.
Speech/Language Impairment (SI/LI)	A communication disorder, such as stuttering, impaired articulation, a language impairment, or a voice impairment, that adversely affects a student's educational performance.
Traumatic Brain Injury (TBI)	An acquired injury to the brain caused by an external physical force or by certain medical conditions such as stroke, encephalitis, aneurysm, anoxia, or brain tumors with resulting impairments that adversely affect a student's educational performance. The term includes open or closed head injuries or brain injuries from certain medical conditions resulting in mild, moderate, or severe impairments in one or more areas, including cognition, language, memory, attention, reasoning, abstract thinking, judgment, problem-solving, sensory, perceptual and motor abilities, psychosocial behavior, physical functions, information processing, and speech. The term does not include injuries that are congenital or caused by birth trauma.
Visual Impairment (VI)	An impairment in vision that, even with correction, adversely affects a student's educational performance. This term includes both partial sight and blindness.

Source: Regulations of the Commissioner of Education, New York State Education Law, Section 4401, Part 200.

Having your child classified as a student with a disability is never an easy process; however, if you understand the criteria by which your child is being evaluated, you will be better able to discuss the options for your child and state a case for one classification over another in your meeting with the CSE. As a parent, you should be aware of the types of programs that are available for your child, particularly if you are looking at a classroom or school where your child can be with age-appropriate peers in language, social skills, and cognitive abilities. If your child is turning 5, it is often difficult to determine how significant his or her developmental delays are or how they will impact your child's learning. Therefore, it is often easier to get the classification of Speech Impaired (assuming your child fits the criteria), since it often describes a young child's more significant disability, but doesn't limit possible placements at such a young age.

It is important to know that a classification may change as a child grows older. This is due to several factors. First, delays in language and fine motor skills are often considered "red flags" for the possibility of learning disabilities. Prior to 1st grade, children are not classified as Learning Disabled (LD), since they have not had any formal classroom experience in learning the skills for reading and math. By the end of 1st grade, however, if a child is struggling with reading, language arts, handwriting, and/or math skills, this may be an indication that he or she could have a learning disability.

A second reason that a child may require a change in classification is due to changes in his or her social-emotional development. As children grow older, they may demonstrate more difficulties in social skills or exhibit more emotional problems. These difficulties are often demonstrated through acting-out behaviors, which become disruptive to the classroom and impact on a child's learning and the learning of the other children in the classroom. The classification of Emotionally Disturbed (ED) also includes children who are emotionally fragile, withdrawn, or socially immature, and therefore require a smaller student/teacher ratio in a classroom setting for learning.

It is understandable that parents are hesitant to have their child classified as ED; however, this is one area where the NYCDOE is more willing to consider a nonpublic school (NPS) placement for a child. In recent years, we have observed some children diagnosed with a Pervasive Developmental Disorder (PDD) and classified as Speech Impaired (SI) when they were younger who often demonstrated significant impairments in their emotional and social skills as they grew older.

There has been an increase in the use of several other classifications in recent years. Other Health Impaired (OHI) is rarely used with younger children unless they are more medically involved or have been diagnosed with a specific medical disorder (i.e., seizure disorder, cerebral palsy, etc.). However, OHI has been used more in the last several years for classifying children with Attention Deficit Disorder (ADD) and Attention Deficit/Hyperactivity Disorder (ADHD).

There are more private special education schools that now accept the classification of Autism (AUT) than in the past. Children who meet the criteria for Autism may also meet the criteria for Speech Impaired (SI) or Emotionally Disturbed (ED). Parents often prefer the classification of Speech Impaired when their child is still young. There are several reasons for this:

1. There are more private schools that accept children classified as SI and ED, but do not accept children who are classified as Autistic.
2. The student populations in these schools can be very different. Schools that accept children with the classification of SI but not Autism generally have peers who are considered more appropriate role models, due to their language, social, and academic abilities.
3. The programs and curriculum in these schools can also be very different. Schools for children with Autism often utilize Applied Behavior Analysis (ABA) in which the student receives 1:1 instruction predominantly throughout the school day. The classrooms have fewer students and tend to be smaller so that distractions can be minimized. This results in the student having limited social interactions with peers on a daily basis. Other schools use a more language-based approach and have more students in the classroom, which can be overstimulating for some children.

As parents, you must keep in mind that a classification is concerned with the area of difficulty that most significantly impacts your child's learning. It also directly relates to the types of related services that your child will receive during the school year. Knowing your child's specific learning and emotional needs will help you to recognize the classification that best characterizes your child.

REFERENCE

Regulations of the Commissioner of Education, New York State Education Law, Section 4401, Part 200.

CHAPTER 4

The IEP

Every student who is receiving special education services or who is approved for these services will receive an Individualized Education Program (IEP). An IEP is a legal document, which means that it is based on an evaluation that identifies your child as having a disability and as needing special education services. Information provided by a child's parents is crucial to a comprehensive outcome.

WHAT IT MEANS TO YOUR CHILD AND YOU

The IEP is the sum of many parts, beginning with an initial evaluation needed to identify relevant information regarding the cognitive, physical, language, developmental, and social-emotional abilities of a child. It determines whether a child is eligible for special education and/or related services, and identifies his/her classification. Projected goals and objectives in each area of need, as well as program modifications and placement, are also written in an IEP.

The IEP will address your child's current level of performance in the following areas: academics and learning, social and emotional skills, and health and physical abilities. Your child's present academic progress is documented, and long- and short-term goals are written for the year. The IEP mandates what services and programs a child will receive and where they will take place. Transportation service (available for all children classified with a disability) is included in a child's IEP as a related service. Beginning at age 5 (or when a child is turning 5), a meeting will be held at least once a year, conducted by the Committee on Special Education (CSE) or your child's special education provider at his/her local public school, to review the most current educational information on your child. The individuals who will be at this meeting form a group called the "Review Team." This group of professionals is assigned by the CSE to consider your child's particular needs and to identify possible recommendations for services and placements.

Prior to the CSE meeting one of the team members, usually a certified social worker (CSW), will schedule a time to observe your child in his/her classroom setting. A report of this observation should be sent to you before you attend the CSE meeting. You may receive a phone call from the CSE before the date they have arranged for your child's IEP meeting, as well as a written notice of your meeting (as required by law). If the date they have given you is not convenient for any reason, you should contact them as soon as possible to request a different date. Do not neglect to call them, as ignoring a written notice may impact on your child's ability to receive services. The goal of the initial CSE meeting is to discuss your child's evaluation and to make an informed group decision to determine if your child has a disability that requires special education services. Subsequent meetings address updates and reviews of your child's IEP and determine whether your child continues to be eligible for special education services.

WHO YOU WILL MEET DURING THE IEP PROCESS

It has been our experience that most of the people engaged in the CSE process are hard-working professionals who apply their best efforts when assessing a child's past and present reports. It is important to keep in mind that most of the individuals are working from knowledge they have collected on paper regarding your child.

You are not required to attend your child's CSE meeting, but we strongly advise that you do. It is up to you to provide information and details that may not be reflected in the paperwork in front of the review team. You should read all your child's evaluations and test information to prepare yourself for the CSE meeting. Since this meeting is a high priority, some families like to bring along a photo of their child in order to put a face to the individual whose life is being discussed. This is your opportunity to participate and be your child's best advocate.

It is required that the CSE meeting include at least a social worker, special education teacher, psychologist, parent member, and general education teacher. The following list of professionals identifies potential participants at your child's CSE meeting:

Social Worker

The social worker is responsible for completing a social history of your child, which is a series of questions that ask you to describe your child's present performance at school, as well as his/her current living situation and health. This is usually done at the district office of the CSE or is sometimes done by telephone. While any of the NYC-

DOE professionals may visit your child's present school to conduct an observation, it is often conducted by the social worker. You should receive a copy of the social history and the classroom observation.

General Education Teacher

This is a teacher with classroom experience in a public school who has knowledge of general education curriculum and the educational skills required for children in the least restricted environment (LRE).

School Psychologist

A school psychologist is a member of the CSE who understands and can explain psychological testing. He/she contributes to the IEP by identifying emotional/social issues and behavior patterns and then plans any psychological services that might be needed for your child. The school psychologist is also responsible for conducting psychological and educational testing to determine your child's eligibility for special education services. This individual will discuss your child's test results at the IEP meeting with you.

Special Education Teacher

This individual will address student–teacher ratio, classroom settings, and specific educational programs available through the NYC-DOE.

Parent Member

A parent member is often referred to as a "parent advocate" who will either attend the meeting in person or be available by telephone during the course of the meeting. This is an individual who has a child with a disability who is receiving special education services. A parent member's presence is intended to give assistance to parents in advocating for their child.

District Representative

This individual, often a social worker, is qualified to provide special education services and is cognizant of the continuum of services and availability of resources in the district. Ultimately the district representative is the person who has the authority to commit to the services that are written in your child's IEP. The district representative may wear two hats in the CSE meeting, and can represent another area of expertise; for example, he/she may also be a school psychologist.

Student

In general we do not recommend that your child attend the IEP meeting, and you should never bring any of your other children, including infants. If you feel that specific information can only be demonstrated by the physical presence of your child, by all means bring him/her to the meeting. Parents should be aware that the CSE team will discuss your child's needs in specific ways, so it may (or may not) be helpful for them to meet your child. In the event that you are attending an IEP meeting for your middle or high school child, assess the information that you perceive will be discussed during the meeting, consult a trusted professional beforehand, and base your decision to include your child accordingly.

Parent or Legal Guardian

. This is a parent, a foster parent, legal guardian, or anyone who has the legal right to make educational decisions for a child, and can sign the IEP on behalf of the child. If you are not the legal parent of a child, you are required to bring legal documentation that gives you the right to sign for decisions relating to a child's education.

Current Teacher or Service Provider

Whether in special education or a regular educational setting, the role of your child's current teacher is extremely important in helping to develop a program that can best address your child's academic and therapeutic needs. The CSE will make every effort to coordinate with the school so that the teacher can be available by telephone at some point in the meeting, if not actually in person. In some cases having a related service provider at the meeting (speech, OT, PT, etc.) is beneficial for addressing the need for additional support/services for your child.

Other

Parents are allowed to bring anyone they want to an IEP meeting (a relative, friend, advocate, attorney, or other professional) who they feel would be able to contribute to the discussion of their child.

At the beginning of the CSE meeting the child's parent or guardian will be asked to sign page two, the conference sheet. This is simply to acknowledge that you attended the meeting—it does not mean that you have agreed with the entire content of the document. Services are agreed upon once you receive the Final Notice of Recommendation by mail. When you sign this form you are agreeing to the recommendations of the IEP for your child. If you do not agree with any portion of the IEP you will have a later opportunity to challenge the IEP, through mediation or through a process called an impartial hearing.

WHEN DOES AN IEP TAKE PLACE?

Every child who receives special education services must have a current IEP by the beginning of each school year; therefore the CSE will typically schedule your child's meeting in the spring of the previous school year. An IEP is updated annually, and every 3 years a triennial evaluation takes place. A triennial evaluation is intended to explore, in greater depth, your child's program and services. At this time an educational and/or psychological evaluation may be required to update your child's progress. This ensures that as your child grows older, he/she continues to be placed in an appropriate educational setting with related services as needed.

WHY AN IEP CAN OR SHOULD BE CHANGED

A child's parent can request a meeting at any time to discuss a possible change or addition to an IEP. Often this is done when a change in a child's program is required, such as when a child is switching schools or requires additional services. As with anything else, your request should be in writing and addressed to the chairperson of your region. If the goals outlined in the IEP are no longer applicable to your child, a change in the IEP may be required to reflect new goals.

CHAPTER 5

Parents' Rights

It is hoped and desired that parents and professionals work together in a mutually supportive and informative way to benefit one person: the child. This is certainly everyone's goal. During this collaboration parents are often at a loss as to what their rights are regarding school placements, recommendations, and services.

GIVING YOUR CONSENT FOR TESTING

Under New York state law you must be notified if a school wishes to conduct testing or an evaluation with the purpose of considering your child for special education services. The nature and purpose of this evaluation must be discussed with you. If your child has never received special education services, your consent is required before testing can be initiated. Once your child has an IEP, your consent for testing is no longer necessary unless additional testing is required. This may happen for an annual review or a triennial (done every 3 years), or for a change in program if the CSE feels that more information is needed to make decisions related to your child's placement or services.

Before conducting a reevaluation, reasonable measures must be taken to obtain consent from the parent. If the CSE is unable to obtain consent, they may proceed with testing of a child without consent. As we have mentioned in Chapter 4, if you disagree with the findings of the evaluation written by the DOE, you can request funding for an independent educational evaluation (IEE). Considering the time involved in this process, it may be more beneficial and less time consuming to find a private evaluator at your own expense.

IEP AND CSE MEETINGS

The first time you consent to an initial evaluation (IE) you should receive a handbook called *Special Education in New York State for Children Ages 3–21: A Parents' Guide.* This can also be ordered from the New

York State Education Department (NYSED) or downloaded from the Web site: *www.nysed.gov*. This handbook provides information about parents' rights and describes the CSE process.

Parents of children with a disability must receive a notice of all proposed meetings related to their child's educational program. You will receive notice before your child's initial evaluation and for each subsequent CSE meeting.

EDUCATIONAL RECORDS

You have the right to request and receive copies of all of your child's educational reports and any material contained in your child's file. Your school district is required to provide these reports no more than 45 calendar days after your request. It is advisable to follow up a telephone request with a written one and, as always, to keep a copy of your contacts with the CSE. If there is information contained in your child's education records that you disagree with or feel is incorrect, you may ask to have this information changed or removed. Again, it would be best to put this request in writing. If necessary, you can request a hearing to address this issue. If you do call, get the name of the person you speak to and ask if you can call him/her directly should there be a delay.

MEDIATION

Mediation is a process provided by New York state education law that is made available to parents of children with disabilities to resolve issues related to any part of the special education process for a child with a disability—evaluation, placement, or provision of services. Mediation is a step considered, prior to an impartial hearing, in order to help resolve disagreements with the school district.

The hope is that mediation will help to resolve any disagreements between parents and the NYCDOE in a timely, nonadversarial manner. Mediation may be requested by a parent or by the Committee on Special Education (CSE). To request mediation in New York City, parents can contact the chairperson for the CSE in your child's school district, or contact the mediation center directly. Every borough has a mediation center known as a Community Dispute Resolution Center Program (CDRCP). Mediation is generally conducted without lawyers. The mediator is not trained in special education and has no legal power to issue a finding or to determine a resolution. Mediators have received training for handling special cases and are skilled in helping each party consider all options available to them.

Any agreement that is reached in mediation will amend your child's IEP and is binding to all parties. Additionally, the CSE is required to meet immediately to update an IEP to make changes agreed upon in mediation. As a parent you can request an impartial hearing at any time, regardless of whether or not you have requested mediation. All discussions within mediation are considered confidential, and a written agreement from mediation cannot be used at an impartial hearing.

A helpful guide to your questions about mediation, *Special Education Mediation: Real Solutions Where Everyone Wins*, can be obtained through the Office of Vocational and Educational Services for Individuals with Disabilities (VESID), which is part of NYSED. You can make a request for mediation through CSE by completing a form provided by the office of your local region. Your request will be forwarded to the local Community Dispute Resolution Center (CDRC), which will assign a mediator and arrange a meeting within 2 weeks of receipt of your request. The CSE may also request mediation, but you should know that mediation is voluntary.

Parents are not responsible for mediation costs. You may bring other people, including a lawyer, but legal fees are not reimbursable. The school district must bring authorized personnel who can enter into agreements related to disputed issues and who are familiar with the disputed issues (including programs) specific to your child's case. Mediation meetings must be scheduled in a timely manner and held at a neutral site that is accessible to all involved. Mediation does not limit or change parents' rights to due process.

We have never known a parent who has chosen to use mediation to solve disputes related to their child's IEP or placement. There are several reasons why this is so. The foremost is time. While mediation is supposed to be timely, the reality of finding a time when everyone can be available is going to delay any mediation. Parents who work outside the home may have difficulty taking time for an IEP meeting. When you add mediation, phone calls, documentation, and a lawyer or other professional contacts, you're talking about a lot more time.

While this is happening, of course, your child is not getting the appropriate services he/she needs. Most parents go directly to an impartial hearing to get the programs and services that their child needs. Mediation does not address reimbursement, which can only be resolved through an impartial hearing.

Parents often become frustrated by the amount of time it takes from the evaluation to the IEP meeting and to placement, which can take as long as four months, and often takes much longer depending on everyone's schedules. In the meantime, your child may not be receiving services, and he/she is losing valuable time in his/her education.

IMPARTIAL HEARINGS

If a parent disagrees with the child's IEP, a request can be made for a legal procedure known as an Impartial Hearing. This request must be made in writing to the NYCDOE, and it is advisable to do so via certified mail with a signed returned receipt. You state the reason you are requesting the hearing, and your proposed solution. It is important to remember to include your child's name and address and the name of his or her current school. Hearings are usually scheduled within a month of a request.

While parents can go to an impartial hearing without legal representation, we strongly recommend that parents retain a lawyer or get help from an advocacy group/agency that is knowledgeable about special education law and the regulations specific to New York state. You may choose to have your child present during the hearing if you feel it would be beneficial to your case. If your child will be attending the hearing, you must notify the impartial hearing officer in advance.

After the impartial hearing officer receives your request, he/she will schedule a date and notify you and the school district in writing. Parents also receive a packet of information, including instructions on how to submit documentation (which must be received at least 5 school days before the hearing). If you want to subpoena other people or documents, information as to how to do so will also be included in the packet you receive. Parents whose primary language is not English can request a translator for the hearing.

A few tidbits about impartial hearings:

- Impartial hearings may be held at the CSE office in the region where your child attends school or at the NYCDOE office at Livingston Street in Brooklyn.
- All hearings are tape-recorded.
- Based on the recent Supreme Court decision (*Schaffer v. Weast*, No. 04–698), parents now bear the "burden of proof," meaning that they must prove that the recommendations

made by the NYCDOE for services and/or programs are not appropriate for their child or that they were not provided in a timely manner. Before this decision, the burden of proof was on the NYCDOE.

- Both the NYCDOE and the parent may present witnesses.
- Everyone (parents, your attorney, the NYCDOE, and the hearing officer) can ask questions of any witness.

At the end of the proceedings the impartial hearing officer is given time to review testimony and will issue a final decision in writing within 15 business days. The NYCDOE is required to complete the process for the impartial hearing within 45 calendar days after receipt of the written request from the parent or the parent's attorney for the hearing.

The NYCDOE and the parent both have the right to appeal the impartial hearing officer's decision to the New York State Review Office of the State Education Department within 30 days from the date of receipt of the decision. The NYCDOE is required to provide information to parents on how to file an appeal.

The cost of an impartial hearing in New York City is approximately $5,000. If parents go to an impartial hearing and wins their case, the NYCDOE must pay the school tuition as well as the parents' legal fees. If parents lose their case, they are responsible for the school tuition, as well as their own legal fees. Parents and the NYCDOE may choose to reach a settlement regarding school placement, in which case the parents pay their legal fees but receive tuition reimbursement (or a percentage of tuition) from the NYCDOE.

PART II

Private School Placement

CHAPTER 6

Getting Into a Private
Special Education School

All parents want the best for their children—the best school, the best teachers, the best services, and the best education. Unfortunately, for children with disabilities the law provides only for an "appropriate education." The choices for parents become very limited, between a few recognized public schools and the private schools that are becoming better known in New York City. Private special education schools are generally categorized as funded or nonfunded. Most of the private schools we have listed are licensed by New York State as nonpublic schools (NPS).

THE DIFFERENCES BETWEEN
PUBLIC SCHOOLS AND PRIVATE SCHOOLS

Public schools are open to all children who reside in New York City. Not all public schools, however, have an appropriate classroom to meet the needs of the children in their neighborhood who have been classified for special education services or programs. Parents are also required to tour other public schools outside of their neighborhood that the CSE feels may be appropriate for their child's needs. This process has led many parents to seek placements at private special education schools, which are referred to as nonpublic schools (NPS).

Private schools that do not accept public funding for students are able to set their own tuition rates. If your child has been accepted by a private, nonfunded school, you will be responsible for paying your child's tuition for the school year. Parents may want to get reimbursed for some or all of your child's tuition through a due process hearing. This is a time-consuming and expensive process, but it is not impossible. It entails documentation describing why a placement at a public school or a nonpublic school is not appropriate for your child. Most parents obtain private evaluations to go along with reports from teachers, therapists, and consultants who have expert knowledge and understanding of their child. It also requires a great deal of time on the parents' part for organizing the written documentation, coordinating the recommendations from each professional, and scheduling meetings with professionals, the NYCDOE, and, possibly, a lawyer.

While we have known a handful of parents who have represented themselves in due process hearings, these parents were extremely knowledgeable about the law and were well prepared to argue their case before the hearing officer. We recommend retaining an attorney to represent your child through what will be a long process. Bear in mind that while you are going through the legal entanglements of this process, you are still required to pay the full tuition for the school year, and any reimbursement from the NYCDOE could take as long as a year. To make matters worse, you will have to go through this process *each year* if your child remains in a nonfunded school and you want to get tuition reimbursement.

Nonpublic schools have been licensed by the New York State Education Department (NYSED) to provide education and services to children identified as having disabilities. As part of the licensing process, the NYSED specifies several criteria for each school:

- Number of classes the school can have and total number of students
- Student–teacher ratios—this can be different based on each classroom, but schools cannot add more students without approval from NYSED
- Classifications the school is licensed to accept
- Therapy services the school can provide
- Tuition rate

These requirements are written into the school's license and cannot be changed without approval from NYSED. If your child is a preschooler who is just entering the CSE process, you should check the classifications that are accepted at the schools as well as the student–teacher ratios. These factors will affect possible placements for your child at specific schools.

Once the school agrees to accept a child who has been approved for NPS, funding for that child is forwarded to the school on a monthly basis. By accepting the child, the school also accepts the IEP recommendations, including the student–teacher ratio and related services.

Parents should be aware that in some circumstances a child's IEP recommendations could be changed in order to qualify for a school placement, since a school does not have to provide services for which it has not been approved. An example of this would be when a student has physical therapy (PT) recommended on his/her IEP, but a school does not provide PT and has no physical therapist on staff. Parents *have to agree* to this change on the IEP if they accept the school. By doing so, the parents understand that physical therapy will not be provided for their child through the school. As part of the agreement with the CSE, the parents will have to agree that they accept the school placement, acknowledging that the school does not provide the therapy service, and will not seek reimbursement from the NYCDOE for the service. In some cases we have known parents who went to a due process hearing to obtain additional therapy services outside the school and were successful in obtaining private therapy after school. A lawyer or advocacy group could best assist you in identifying whether such legal action would be appropriate or not.

TUITION

A primary difference among schools is tuition. Public schools are obviously free; nonpublic schools have tuition rates set by the NYSED that are accepted as tuition payment for any child referred by the CSE; and independent private schools can set their own tuition rate each year. Tuition is paid directly to the NPS by the NYCDOE for children they have accepted once the IEP is approved by the state. In private schools where funding is not accepted, parents are responsible for paying tuition for their children, of which all or a percentage may be reimbursed by the NYCDOE. A few parents we know have chosen to pay tuition for a private school and not be reimbursed, preferring not to become involved with the NYCDOE. Most parents will attempt to obtain reimbursement of at least part of the tuition through a due process hearing.

FINDING A PRIVATE SCHOOL
FOR YOUR CHILD

We believe that you should trust your intuition as to whether a school is right for your child, based on your knowledge and understanding of his/her cognitive, language, social-emotional, and physical needs. Once you have toured a school and received answers to your questions, you should organize the information so that it is easy for you to use.

The following is a list of questions that may help you in determining whether a private school can best address your child's needs.

1. What is the profile of the school and classrooms?
   - What is the philosophy of the school? Does it fit with your own philosophy of educating children?
   - What are the student–teacher ratios?
   - What do you observe about children's learning styles and abilities in the classrooms?

2. What's happening in the classroom?
   - Is the classroom well organized?
   - Are there a variety of materials and sufficient materials available for all the children?
   - Is the classroom print-rich? Are there words/sentences, classroom information, and children's work on the walls or placed in view around the classroom?
   - Is there active learning incorporated into the classroom (hands-on, experiential, manipulatives)? Are materials easily accessible to children?
   - Can you identify the curriculum being used? Does it appear to be appropriate for the age and grade level of the children?
   - How are children learning—in small groups, large groups, independently?
   - What is the noise level in the classroom? Are there other sensory concerns relevant to your child?

3. What are your impressions of the teacher(s) and assistant teacher(s)?
   - How does the teaching staff interact with the children?
   - Does the teaching staff act professionally toward each other?
   - Does the classroom teaching style fit your child's learning style?
   - What alternative strategies does the teacher use?
   - How are behaviors handled?
   - Do the teachers seem happy and enthusiastic when teaching?

4. What do you observe about the students in the classrooms?
   - Are the students similar to your child in cognitive, language, social-emotional, and physical skills?
   - Are there children in the classroom with significant behavior difficulties?
   - Do the children appear interested and involved in the lessons and activities?
   - Do the children seem happy in their classroom environment?

5. What other settings were you able to observe within the school (cafeteria, therapy rooms, bathrooms, outdoor play space)?
   - Where are they located in relation to the classrooms?
   - What is expected in terms of children moving from one place to another?
   - Is the school accessible to children and parents who have physical disabilities?
   - How many classes/children may be participating in each setting?
   - What types of sensory issues would you anticipate in each setting for your child?

6. What other information about school policies would you want to know?
   - What kind of communication with administrators and teachers/therapists can you expect?
   - How often are conferences held during the school year?
   - How can you request meetings with staff or administrators?
   - Are teachers, therapists, or other staff members available to speak to parents before, during, or after the end of the school day?
   - How can parents become involved in classroom activities and in school events?
   - How does the school want parents to be involved? Is there a PTA?
   - Does the school provide workshops for parents?
   - Is there an afterschool program?
   - How will the school help you in finding the next school/placement for your child?

It helps to put together your own list, one that specifically relates to your child's needs. There may be certain conditions that you require for your child that are a priority, and other issues that you can compromise on. Don't fully rely on a school's administrative staff to determine if a school is the best fit for your child. As a parent you have a broader view than anyone else when considering your child's best school placement. Getting your child into private school requires a lot of energy and focus initially, although the process can be streamlined to the extent that you can address your search to issues that are most relevant to your child and family.

CHAPTER 7

The Application Process

Coordinating an evaluation for your child, going on school tours, and completing the application process has become a full-time job for many parents. Since school tours begin in the fall, you should give yourself 1 year to start the application process. The application process should begin with a conversation with your child's school director, teachers, and therapists. With their guidance you can focus on contacting the schools that will best suit your child's specific needs. This conversation should occur during the school year prior to applying to new schools.

WHAT'S NEEDED, WHEN IT'S NEEDED,
AND WHO TO TALK TO

Prior to September, you should schedule an evaluation for your child so that the written report will be available for application packets and deadlines for submission to private schools. You might want to consider contacting schools in the spring to obtain information about applying for your child and to ask when you should call about school tours for the next school year. Collect as much information about as many schools as soon as possible. Most schools will have some type of brochure you can request; checking a school's Web site is another way to obtain more information.

The next step is to schedule a date for a school tour. You may request an application form at that time, or you may have to wait until the school tour. It is never too early to receive applications; you need only pay an application fee should you choose to send in the application. Fees vary from school to school, but typically are in the range of $50 to $200.

The initial phone call you make to a school is the beginning of the application process. Be prepared, be concise, and be unfailingly courteous. You are not an anonymous voice. You will be remembered, for better or for worse, by your first contact with the school. While this can be a stressful time for families, you should not allow any anxiety that you might be experiencing to translate into rudeness or impatience. Have pen and paper at hand to take down whatever information they give you and be prepared to answer a few simple questions, such as your child's date of birth, gender, present school, home address, and telephone number. You may be asked to describe your child's particular learning issues, but this is not the time to discuss your child's special needs in detail. That will come later, should you choose to tour the school and begin the application process.

THE APPLICATION

When completing application forms, be aware that schools will have different deadlines for their return. The smart approach obviously would be to fill out the ones with the shortest deadlines first. Application deadlines are not flexible, they are definite. It is very important that you commit to getting them completed and received by the schools on time. Hand-delivering your application is one way to ensure its timely arrival, particularly when you are uncomfortably close to the deadline. Sending it with a signed receipt will assure that the school has received it. A follow-up phone call a few days later to ask if the school has received your child's packet is recommended. It is very important to make a copy of the entire application before it is sent to a school.

WHAT TO INCLUDE IN YOUR CHILD'S APPLICATION PACKET

As soon as you know what schools you intend to apply to for your child, you should approach your child's teachers and therapists and ask them to write a current report on your child. Classroom reports should include your child's strengths, what your child has mastered during the year, and what he/she is currently working on. Make sure you request this information as early as possible, and agree upon a time frame for its return. All of this will need to be coordinated with the director of your child's school. If your child's current school has told you that they have forwarded the requested reports to a school, you should contact the school to make sure they have received everything for your child's packet several weeks prior to the deadline.

Your child's current school will probably be asked to complete a questionnaire about his/her academic skills, classroom behaviors, and social-emotional development. This form is returned directly to the school to become part of a child's application packet. Parents should not ask to get a copy of this information, as it is considered confidential between the schools. However, you *should* check that the school has received this information.

While you are completing your child's application, you should contact friends and family members who may know anyone whose child attends the school or who works at the school. They may be willing to speak on behalf of you and your child, particularly regarding your contribution to the school (i.e., fundraising, parent involvement, etc.).

Finally, it is up to you to keep track of the information you need and to anticipate the timeline involved for reports to be written and returned to you well before application deadlines. Most schools require that all information including therapist's reports be sent at the same time as the application. Returning an incomplete application by the required date, and sending the delayed reports later, is a situation you want to avoid. This not only makes a poor first impression, it creates an unnecessary delay in the processing of your child's application.

The following checklist can be used as a guide to help you organize the application materials that you'll need for most schools:

1. Cover letter
2. Application, including release form
3. Current evaluations
4. Current classroom report
5. Current therapy/related services reports
6. Current IEP
7. Application fee
8. Reports from other outside professionals
9. Photo of your child
10. Other possible documents—developmental history, tuition/financial aid forms, and so on

Remember to make a copy of all of the above and attach a page that clearly shows you at a glance:

• The name of the school
• The deadline date for the application
• The date you sent the application (attach receipt)
• The date current reports from teachers/therapists were sent
• The date you contacted the school regarding receipt of application and the person you spoke to

CHAPTER 8

School Tours and Interviews

Each school will have its own timetable for school tours, but tours typically start in the fall. When preparing to visit a school, remember that you will be making an impression as a parent during your short time there.

APPROPRIATE AND INAPPROPRIATE BEHAVIORS (OF PARENTS)

In our experiences we have found that not everyone seems to know what is acceptable or unacceptable behavior when taking a tour of a school. Here are a few helpful reminders for parents:

- *Be on time.* Tours are carefully planned and timed by the school to fit into the flow of a particular day. The administration must take into account many factors, not the least of it keeping the interruption of the school day at a minimum. Lateness shows a lack of consideration for this process, and it may not be possible to join a group that has already left.
- *Do not bring children.* A school tour is not the place to bring children of any age.
- *Turn off all beepers and cellphones.* Your priority is to focus on the task at hand: touring the school. The use of cellphones and beepers creates more than a distraction; it conveys rudeness and a lack of respect for others.
- *Be prepared.* Bring a notepad and several pens. Familiarize yourself in advance with the mission and policies of the school you are touring. Note the name of the person who conducts the tour so you can send him/her a personal note of thanks afterwards.
- *Be courteous and considerate.* Don't talk or linger in a classroom after your guide has led the group away, as this is disruptive to the children. Don't ask excessive questions, limiting the opportunity for other parents to ask their own.

WHAT TO ASK

We also believe that you should be prepared to ask a few questions that will be relevant to your child's application to a school. Some questions that come to mind are:

> What classifications does the school accept?
> What training do the teachers have?
> What is the student–teacher ratio in each classroom?
> When will you be informed of the school's decision?
> How will you be informed (i.e., by phone call or letter)?
> What therapy does the school provide?
> What is the length of the school day?
> How does the school handle snack, lunch, and food issues?
> What afterschool programs are available?
> What is the extent of parent involvement?
> Is there a parent association?
> What curriculum does the school use in the classroom?
> What schools do graduating students go to?

WHAT DEFINITELY *NOT* TO ASK!

There are also some questions that parents should *not* ask while part of a school tour. We have listed a few of these below:

> How will the school work specifically with my child?
> How does the school handle aggressive behavior? (They may think that you're talking about your child's behavior.)
> What are the issues concerning [a child you saw during the tour]? (All information regarding children is confidential.)
> What are the bus schedules and travel times for the school? (Schools are not responsible for busing, but they will work with parents on transportation once a child is accepted.)

When visiting a school, pay close attention to your instincts. If your child is accepted, you will be spending a good amount of time there as well. The location of the school is obviously important. Proximity to your home means shorter travel time for your child as well as the opportunity for forming friendships with other children who attend the school and live in your community. However, this is not always an option, so balance that factor against other positives if the school you like is not conveniently located. Soak in the atmosphere. Your impression of the environment and your instincts about the administration and staff will help you decide whether your child and family will benefit and thrive in that setting.

PREPARING YOURSELF AND YOUR CHILD

Schools set up appointments for interviews very carefully in order to fit the time schedules of their staff and the structure of the school day. You should know that if you are unable to bring your child on the day scheduled, your child might not be given a second opportunity for an interview.

Each school has its own method when it comes to interviewing children. If possible, find out in advance what type of interview they conduct—one-on-one with an adult or time in a classroom with other students. As a parent, it is important that you prepare your child for a school interview without creating unnecessary anxiety in either of you. You'll know if it's best to discuss specifics about the interview with your child. Who they will meet, what they will do, and how long it will take are details that may be helpful for him/her to know.

When you speak with a school to arrange the details of your child's interview, listen carefully to the information you are given. If there are questions you have directly related to the interview that haven't been addressed, ask them at this time. Do not talk at length about what the school might anticipate from your child during the interview. Special education professionals have seen many children (and many behaviors) and understand that a child may not be at his/her best during an interview. It has been our experience that schools try to make children feel as comfortable as possible throughout this process.

You should not anticipate your child's behavior during a school interview or assume that he or she will respond in the same way that you have observed in the past. You may be tempted to overly prepare your child or call the school beforehand to give them "hints" on how to interact with your child. While you may feel you are being helpful and proactive, this is not always the case. Let your child's behavior during the interview speak for itself. Keep in mind that the professionals in special education schools are well aware that the interview process is a stressful one for parents and children.

The following are our recommendations for parents concerning what to do and what not to do regarding their child's school interview.

Do:

- Ask how long the interview will be and where it will take place. Will your child be working with one adult in an office, or joining a classroom with other students?
- Ask what your child will be doing so you can prepare him or her ahead of time.
- Ask if you should provide lunch or a snack.
- Get the name(s) of the school staff your child will be meeting with and tell your child who they are a day before the interview.
- Give the school a contact number where you can be reached during the time of the interview in case you are expected to leave the school premises.
- Be prompt and leave your child at the school soon after you arrive. Prolonging your goodbye will only make your child more anxious about the interview.
- Be aware that your child may be overwhelmed at the end of an interview, so limit your questioning about the interview. You don't want your child to be reluctant to go to the next one.
- Attempt to schedule school interviews at intervals so your child doesn't attend them back-to-back.
- Follow up your child's interview immediately with a handwritten thank-you note to the school.

Don't:

- Allow your anxieties regarding your child's performance to spill over into conversations you have with him or her regarding the school interview.
- Tell the school that you are anxious about any part of the interview process; this will send a red flag to them regarding your child.
- Overprepare your child—a simple conversation the day before is enough.
- Call the school during your child's interview unless they tell you to.
- Call the school many times to ask "if they have made a decision" regarding your child's placement
- Show up early to pick up your child and ask if your child is "finished yet."
- Ask the interviewer specific questions about how the interview went in front of your child. It is unprofessional for a teacher or other member of the school's staff to discuss your child's interview at that time.

If you are contacted for a parent interview you will obviously want to make a favorable impression. Be on time, be prepared, and be calm! The interview will usually not be more than an hour and will involve more specific questions about your child and family. At this point the school wants to know that you are going to be supportive of your child and his/her educational program at the school. They may want to discuss what your goals and priorities are for your child, and how you will be expected to participate in your child's education if he/she is accepted.

During the interview you should also demonstrate your interest in the school's parent association, special events, and fundraising. The reality is that most of these schools depend on fundraising to cover the difference between the tuition they receive and the costs of educating their students. It's a reality for nearly every school. It is here where you can help make an awkward situation less so by indicating an understanding and desire to contribute your time to help the school meet its obligations.

Finally, the school wants to know that you will be an integral part of their community and will be continuously involved in your child's education. They want to know that you are a parent who feels committed to the school's mission and programs and that you can be counted on to assist in providing the best educational program for your child.

CHAPTER 9

The Decision

Touring schools, completing applications, taking your child on interviews, making follow-up phone calls, and writing letters is an arduous test of endurance, but now the really hard part begins—waiting to hear from the schools. In general, schools will contact parents within 2 weeks of interviewing a child, but you should ask each school during your tour or interview when you could expect a decision.

There are different factors that a school balances when considering a child's application. Schools are looking for a child who can meet the academic expectations of their program and who can benefit from and contribute to the socialization skills in a classroom. The admissions committee looks for children who are similar in cognitive, language, and emotional skills when creating new classrooms. Since there are usually more boys applying to special education schools than girls, gender balance is sometimes a significant factor, although by no means would it be the only one.

SCHOOL ACCEPTANCE OR REJECTION

If your child is accepted to a school you will most likely receive a phone call from the admissions director. Some schools will call to tell you that they are unable to place your child; others will send a letter. If you are notified by mail that there was no place for your child, it will most likely be a form letter. The letter is unlikely to provide any specific reasons as to why your child was not accepted by the school.

At this point, it may be helpful to place a call to the school. The purpose of this call is not to plead your case, but to gather information. There are several reasons for making a phone call to a school. First, you want to determine the reasons why your child was not offered a place. Ask the admissions director if he/she can provide more detail as to why your child was not offered a place. Second, you should ask if your child might be an appropriate candidate for a future placement (at middle- or high-school age).

If you are told there was not an appropriate classroom for your child, ask about a waiting list. It is rare, but it does happen that a school accepts a child from a waiting list. For example, a child who has been accepted may be unable to attend because his or her family has moved. The acceptance of a child from a waiting list can happen at any time; a school may contact a family on the waiting list even after the school year has begun. In such a situation, parents will have to make a quick decision concerning whether they are willing to remove their child from his/her current school or take a chance that the waiting list's school will have a spot the following year.

As hard as it might be to accept, if a school tells you that it does not feel your child would be accepted in the future, it is doing you a favor. Parents often apply for several years in a row to the same school. There is nothing wrong with doing this in most cases. If you are going to re-apply, you should do it with the knowledge that the school feels your child would be appropriate given different circumstances. It is useless to apply over and over again when the school has decided that it does not anticipate that your child would be appropriate for the school.

If your child has not been accepted, keep focused and stay balanced. When your child is not accepted to your school of choice, it can be very stressful; options feel limited, and parents often feel that they need to pull out the stops on behalf of their child. As frustrating as it may be, no amount of indignation or pleading is going to help your child.

A productive alternative would be to ask the admissions director if he/she could recommend another school where your child would be a good match. Admissions directors are very knowledgeable of other schools and can be helpful in pointing you in the right direction. They also may know which schools have openings.

If you have not found a school to accept your child, don't panic. There are several options. If your child is currently in a nonpublic school (NPS), one option is to ask the school to request a waiver from the NYSED. This is possible only if your child is "aging out" (turning 5 years of age) of his/her current school and you have not been able to secure a placement for your child in another school. It is up to your child's present school to decide if they can do this, as they need to consider several factors. First, the classroom in which your child would remain must conform to the 36-month age span that is allowed in special education classroom settings. This means that there cannot be more than 36 months of age difference between the youngest and the oldest student in a classroom. Furthermore, the school must decide whether your child will be best served by remaining at the school for another year and whether they can continue to provide an appropriate program for your child. In either case, a waiver is allowed for only 1 year. NYSED may not agree to the waiver, in which case you may have to ask for an impartial hearing to secure a placement and services.

Should you be in the fortunate position of having your child accepted at more than one school, you will want to consider which school is most appropriate for your child, how conveniently located each school is, what grade levels are supported, and whether there is a 10- month or 12-month (summer) program. If both schools are equally desirable, you should talk to them and see what additional information you can obtain to help you reach a decision.

SWITCHING SCHOOLS

While many of you will be thrilled that a school has accepted your child, you also have to keep in mind that you may be faced with the same application process within a few years. Unfortunately, many elementary schools only go through 5th or 6th grade. If your child's new school has eight grades or high school, you will have more time, or may never have to consider another school application again!

Most schools have a process for students to transition to their next school. As a parent, you may feel that your child is ready to move earlier than you or the school had anticipated. It is best to work with your child's school during this period, as you will depend on their expertise and professional connections in getting into the next school of your choice.

The transition to a new school occurs more naturally from elementary to middle school or from middle school to high school. This is the time when more openings will be available as other children move to new schools. Occasionally a placement becomes available between grades, but this is rare. It is best not to discuss moving to a new school with your child until you have had the chance to speak to teachers and other professionals to get their input.

Most parents have conferences with their child's teachers and therapists at least twice a year to discuss the progress that their child is making. This is the best time to approach the professionals who work with your child if you are intending to look at new schools. You should speak to the director of your child's school first to initiate this discussion. The people who work directly with your child will have their own opinions of your child's readiness to move to another school.

PREPARING YOURSELF AND YOUR CHILD

As children mature, they should be better able to understand changes that occur, including going to a new school. With children who have special needs, using experiences from their lives (i.e., when they left preschool) is often helpful. When children ask questions about why they have to leave a school, respond positively, using language that they can understand. If you have difficulty or are unsure as to how to talk to your child about this, ask teachers and therapists for assistance. They can often work with your child within the classroom or therapy settings to encourage discussion about such an important event. This should occur naturally when other children in the classroom are moving, too.

If your child is moving to another nonpublic school, funding for tuition will usually be transferred to the new school. This must be done through the CSE. You will be required to attend a meeting regarding the change in schools, as it is considered a change in your child's program.

If you choose to transfer your child within the school year, funding may become difficult. This will depend on several factors, including your child's current functioning, whether the new school is a private nonfunded school or another NPS, and whether your child's current school feels that the new school is more appropriate for your child. Obviously, if your child's current school agrees with the move, it should make the change easier.

We recommend that parents work with their child's current school in determining the best time for a change in placement. You will also need the assistance of the school director, teachers, and therapists, who are usually familiar with other schools, to help you with reports and other documentation required for a new school. These professionals can often pave the way so that the move is successful for both your child and you.

PART III

School Profiles

Our purpose in writing this section is to give you an accurate profile of each school with enough information to assist you in choosing a school for your child. One or both of us visited each school, where we interviewed school administrators and staff and toured their classrooms and facilities. The information included in this section was based on questions that most parents ask in order to determine if a school is appropriate for their child. The school profiles are by no means comprehensive. Each school could fill several additional pages with more specific details about their program, curriculum, and unique perspective on children with disabilities. Every school will be able to provide extensive information to you through their tours, brochures, and application packets. However, after reviewing the schools in this guide, you should be able to identify the ones that would best meet your own child's needs. We hope this is helpful in your quest to finding the best educational setting for your child.

The Aaron School

309 East 45th Street
New York, NY 10017
Phone: (212) 867–9594
Fax: (212) 867–9864
Director: Debra Schepard
Admissions: Linda Gardner
Web site: *info@aaronschool.org*

Grades: Pre-K–Grade 5

School Year Program: 10 Month

Age Range of Students: 4–12 years

Funded for NYC: No

Enrollment: 91

Summer Program: Yes

School Region: 9

Tuition: $35,000

Financial Assistance: Low-interest loans are provided through School and Student Service (SSS) for Financial Aid and are based on family income.

Classifications Accepted: Speech Impaired (SI), Learning Disabled (LD), Other Health Impaired (OHI) including Attention Deficit Disorder (ADD)

The Aaron School will also consider children who have average or higher cognitive skills and who have difficulties in sensory or auditory processing and social and pragmatic skills.

Related Services: Speech Therapy, Occupational Therapy, and Counseling (on a limited basis), Learning Specialist

Student–Teacher Ratios: Aaron has a transition kindergarten with a student–teacher ratio of 8–10:1:1. In kindergarten through grade 5, the ratio is generally 10:1:1 and 12:1:1. Some classes have an additional adult depending on the needs of the class.

Classroom Placement and Instruction: Students are placed in classes based on their academic functioning and social levels. There is never more than 2 years between the ages in each class. Reading and math groups are scheduled at the same time each day so that small groups can focus on individual skills. Aaron uses Orton-Gillingham and Wilson Fundations for reading. For those children who have difficulty with phonics, the teachers also use the Bank Street Readers to introduce sight words. Handwriting skills are taught using Handwriting Without Tears. In math, children are introduced to Stern Structural Mathematics, which includes hands-on manipulatives for learning. A science curriculum is being developed by Aaron; however, the teachers use programs (Real Science/SRA) that primarily involve activities and experiments. Social studies is also based on the NYS Learning Standards.

The art program at Aaron includes art history as well as drawing, painting, and crafts. The school has an art room and ceramic studio. Music is provided once a week and includes singing, movement, and rhythm activities. Adaptive physical education (APE) is taught by a movement specialist who incorporates yoga, balance and strength, movement, and sports skills into class activities.

The Aaron School has also created a social skills curriculum that they are implementing within each classroom. As part of this curriculum, the speech therapists spend time in classrooms working with children within social situations, assisting them in negotiating and problem-solving, and with language related to emotions. The school has initiated an Affinity Program with students 8 years and above where administrators spend 30 minutes each week involved with students' interests/passions (i.e., architecture).

Aaron has a computer lab, library, gymnasium, and sensory gym. The students use a local park for outdoor play and bring their own lunch, which they eat in the classroom. During the summer, students have access to a pool for swimming.

Summer Program: Aaron has a 6-week summer program that focuses on a theme. Reading and math skills are reinforced through small groups in the morning and field trips and swimming are provided in the afternoons. Mandated therapies for students are maintained during the summer program.

Afterschool Programs: Drama/theater, directed by a teacher/artist, sports, martial arts, ceramics, and clubs are available in the afterschool program as well as social skills groups.

Parent Involvement: The school sponsors several family events throughout the school year in which parents are involved. Aaron has a Parent Association that also organizes fundraising, school events, and an annual book fair.

Parent/Family Services: Aaron School has a range of services for parents and families. Individual counseling is available with the school psychologist upon request. Support groups are held on Fridays during the school day. Workshops are conducted in the evenings and include speakers in areas of interest to parents.

School Tours: Weekly tours are given to parents throughout the school year. Parents can schedule a tour by calling the admissions director for an appointment.

The Application: The application can be obtained during a tour of the school, or you can request one by calling the school. The application must be completed, including all required documentation and the application fee, in order for your child to be considered for placement.

The admissions coordinator and school psychologist will review the application and request an interview with you and your child if they feel that your child would benefit from Aaron's program. During the interview, your child will be informally assessed and you will meet with the director.

Parents are notified shortly after the interview regarding their child's acceptance to Aaron. When a child is accepted at Aaron, parents are required to sign a contract and place a deposit in order to secure their child's place for the next school year. The Aaron School accepts children throughout the year for the following school year.

Application Fee: $100

Association for Metroarea
Autistic Children, Inc. (AMAC)

25 West 17th Street
New York, NY 10011
Phone: (212) 645–5005
Fax: (212) 645–0170
Executive Director: Frederica Blausten
Director of Education: Felicia Blumberg
E-mail: rica@amac.org
Web site: *www.amac.org*

Grades: Pre-K–Grade 8   **Enrollment:** 108

School Year Program: 12 Month   **Summer Program:** Yes

Age Range of Students: 5–16 years   **School Region:** 9

Funded for NYC: Yes

Tuition: Free for students placed through school districts.

Financial Assistance: N/A

Classifications Accepted: Autistic (AUT), Emotionally Disturbed (ED), Speech Impaired (SI), Pervasive Development Disorder (PDD), and Asperger's Disorder Syndrome (AS)

Related Services: Occupational Therapy, Physical Therapy, Speech, Counseling, and Applied Behavior Analysis

Student–Teacher Ratios: 1:1, 6:1:3, 8:1:2, 10:1:1

Classroom Placement and Instruction: AMAC classes are formed based on several factors, including social skills, language, reciprocity, and ability. There are three levels of classrooms at AMAC. The Special Needs Unit (SNU) has a class size of 6:1:3. Instruction in this class is primarily one-to-one, supplemented with group instruction. Applied behavior analytic teaching is used in the areas of early academics and communication and self-help skills. Communication Acquisition Needs (CAN) has a class size of 8:1:2. Students are divided into groups of four, supplemented by one-to-one teaching to support developing skills as well as to give support to skills that are not developing as expected.

Team Ten has a class size of 10:1:1. This class is taught entirely within a group setting, with the goal to transition students into a less restrictive setting in their community schools. AMAC uses Applied Behavior Analysis (ABA) techniques to address students' individual needs. A variety of curriculum programs are used for all content areas.

The school has a small library, a music room, a computer room, and a gymnasium; the children eat their lunch in the classroom. AMAC has a Reward Store, and students have the opportunity to earn bracelets throughout the school day that they can later redeem for items at the store.

Summer Program: AMAC has a summer camp available in August for children ages 5 and up. It is located in Utica, New York, and the children receive the same type of individualized care with staff who are all trained in ABA. The camp offers swimming and activities in the areas of social skills, creative arts, and therapeutic recreation.

Afterschool Programs: AMAC offers an afterschool program 3 to 5 days a week to teach computer skills, arts and crafts, social skills, music, and movement. A Saturday program is available for children through age 14.

Parent Involvement: The school sends home written communication each day, and parents call to schedule meetings with teachers or to schedule a classroom observation.

Parent/Family Services: AMAC has a parent support group during the day, and workshops are offered in the evenings on various subjects including Behavior Modification Training.

School Tours: Parents must call AMAC to schedule an appointment for a school tour.

The Application: An application can be mailed upon request at the intake appointment. Parents should submit their child's current IEP if AMAC's program is appropriate for your child.

Application Fee: None

Brooklyn Blue Feather Elementary Association for the Help of Retarded Children (AHRC)

477 Court Street
Brooklyn, NY 11231
Phone: (718) 834–0597
Fax: (718) 834–0768
Principal: Joseph Cordasco

Grades: Nongraded

Enrollment: 128

School Year Program: 12 Month

Summer Program: Yes

Age Range of Students: 5–11 years

School Region: 8

Funded for NYC: Yes

Tuition: All tuition is received from funding for children through CSE

Financial Assistance: N/A

Classifications Accepted: Autistic (AUT), Emotionally Disturbed (ED), Other Health Impaired (OHI), Multiple Disabilities (MD)

Related Services: Occupational Therapy, Physical Therapy, Speech Therapy, and Counseling

Student–Teacher Ratios: 8:1:1, 8:1:4

Classroom Placement and Instruction: There are 17 classrooms at the Blue Feather Elementary School. Children are grouped by age and ability level within a 36-month margin. Some children have paras in the classroom. The teachers are all trained in Applied Behavior Analysis (ABA), which is the instructional program utilized in all classrooms. Other programs used are TEACCH Methodology, Verbal Behavior, Incidental Learning, and Task Analysis.

If mandated by a child's IEP, speech and OT services are provided in the classroom. The school has a library/media room with traditional as well as touch-screen computers. The children receive computer lessons two times a week. There is a small gym and an outdoor yard area. Blue Feather has created a "Snoezelen" Room, which is a multisensory room used to increase positive behaviors for individuals and to promote sensory development and hand–eye coordination, language development, and relaxation. Yoga instruction is included for students. The children at Blue Feather go on field trips in the surrounding neighborhood as well as bowling trips several times a year. Children eat in a lunchroom located on the premises of the school.

There is a full-time registered nurse and certified social worker on staff. The school follows the New York City Board of Education calendar.

Summer Program: There is a 2-week summer camp in late August in Columbia County in upstate New York, as well as a 6-day camp for 5- to 12-year-olds in upstate New York.

Parent Involvement: Parents are encouraged to be active participants in their children's education through parent training, offered twice a month. There is a parent teacher organization at Blue Feather.

Parent/Family Services: The social worker conducts a parent support group along with a psychologist. Additional services such as respite, counseling, summer camp, mental heath, and medical services are all available as needed.

School Tours: Parents should call the principal to request an individual or a group appointment.

The Application: Parents must complete a two-page application form. Children are screened only after the CSE recommends a placement at the school. Blue Feather requires all evaluations and a current IEP.

Application Fee: None

The Child School

587 Main Street
Roosevelt Island, NY 10044
Phone: (212) 223–5055
Fax: (212) 223–5031
Director: Maari de Souza
Web site: *www.thechildschool.org*

Grades: K–Grade 12   **Enrollment:** 134

School Year Program: 10 Month   **Summer Program:** yes

Age Range of Students: 5–14 years   **School Region:** 2

Funded for NYC: Yes

Tuition: $22,874 (school year); $3,812 (6-week summer program)

Financial Assistance: N/A

Classifications Accepted: Learning Disability (LD), Speech and Language Impaired (SLI), Emotionally Disturbed (ED), Asperger's Syndrome (AS)

Related Services: Speech Therapy, Occupational Therapy, and Counseling

Student–Teacher Ratios: The elementary school (K–6th grade) has nine classes with a student–teacher ratio of 6:1:1 and 8:1:1. The middle school has five classes with a ratio of 12:1:1.

Classroom Placement and Instruction: Instruction is very individualized at the Child School, depending on each student's needs for both reading and mathematics. The elementary school is comprised of Forms 1–9, which includes students ranging from kindergarten to grade 6. Students are grouped in Forms within a 36-month age range, based on an individual assessment conducted by a teacher at the beginning of the admissions process. The curriculum includes readiness skills, reading, math, language arts, typing, social studies, Spanish, science, and computer science. The Child School uses a behavior modification system to provide students with strategies to help them self-monitor personal behavior.

    Music is an integral part of the curriculum at the Child School. Students who have a special interest and ability can elect to perform in an ensemble or join the Child School chorus. Through their creative arts therapy program, the staff and students produce and act in an end-of-the–year June play. Also, students have the opportunity to express themselves creatively and enhance their public speaking, writing, and comprehension skills in the media lab, which includes the school's own radio and TV station.

Students are offered a variety of age-appropriate adaptive physical education activities through the school year; there is also an extracurricular varsity program in team sports such as basketball, softball, cheerleading, and track at the Child School.

A unique aspect to the Child School is the many field trips that are available to the students throughout the school year, some of which are overseas.

Facilities at the Child School include science and media labs, a gymnasium, a cafeteria, a swimming pool, a professionally equipped stage, a library with computer stations, an art room, and a music room. There is access to outdoor playgrounds and sports playing fields on the grounds, as well as a courtyard with an organic garden.

Special features of the Child School include a mock apartment on campus, for use in personal independence courses; a school kitchen with an adjacent restaurant; and a school store.

Summer Program: A 6-week summer program is available for an additional cost of $3,812. The summer trips are chosen based on what the students are learning in summer school.

Afterschool Programs: Afterschool programs include a homework club, sports clubs, band practice, and chorus.

Parent Involvement: The Child School has a parent association called Parents and Teachers Together (PTT) that meets regularly throughout the school year. Parents volunteer to work with the school for activities such as the annual play and fundraising.

Parent/Family Services: Counseling is offered to parents, as well as workshops during the school year. Some workshops are intended to provide parents with support techniques toward understanding and responding effectively to their child's performance and behavior at home, to help with homework, and to encourage communication between parents and the school administration.

School Tours: Parents should call the school to arrange a tour and to meet with the director.

The Application: Call the school for an application.

Application Fee: $50

The Churchill School

301 East 29th Street
New York, NY 10016
Phone: (212) 722–0610
Fax: (212) 722–1387
Head: Kristy Baxter
Admissions: Wendy Federico
E-mail: wfederico@churchillschool.com
Web site: *www.churchillschool.com*

Grades: K–Grade 12

Enrollment: 396

School Year Program: 10 Month

Summer Program: No

Age Range of Students: 5–18.7 years

School Region: 9

Funded for NYC: Yes

Tuition: $31,000

Financial Assistance: Yes, as determined by the School and Student Service (SSS) for Financial Aid and at the discretion of the Head of the school.

Classifications Accepted: Learning Disabled (LD), Speech Impaired (SI)

Related Services: Counseling, Speech Therapy, Occupational Therapy

Student–Teacher Ratios: 12:1:1

Classroom Placement and Instruction: Churchill's educational program provides a learning environment for students who are described as having language or reading difficulties, attention problems, and perceptual and/or motor issues. Classes are nongraded from kindergarten through grade 5. In grades 6–12, students are placed in small groups for instruction, which includes multisensory strategies, repetition, and reinforcement of skills. Classes are created based on a combination of factors including a student's age, cognitive and language abilities, reading and math levels, and social skills.

In the elementary school at Churchill, reading and math are taught in small groups of 5 to 6 students. The writing program is designed for students who have language-based learning difficulties. Churchill has created its own social studies and science curricula, which are taught within the whole class setting. Health, physical education, library, and computers are integrated within each student's educational program. Departmentalization begins in the middle school at Churchill. Language arts (including expository writing) and math skills continue to be taught, while organizational and study skills are emphasized for students. Social studies and science are project-based, with a focus on research skills. As with the younger students, health, physical education, library science, and computers are included in each student's program. Churchill offers a high school curriculum through which students may obtain a Regents, local, or IEP diploma.

Churchill has well-equipped modern facilities, including two computer labs, a library, a large gymnasium, a cafeteria, a garden, three art rooms, and a roof playground. The arts program at Churchill includes fine arts, crafts, drama/theater, and dance. The school also has music as well as a high school band. Horticulture is a unique program that has been added to the curriculum for older students.

Afterschool Programs: Afterschool activities at Churchill are planned by the parents association. Art, music, chess, swimming, "mad science," rollerblading, mime, martial arts, and yoga have been introduced to students as part of the afterschool program. Churchill also has sports teams that compete with other independent schools in the metropolitan area.

Parent Involvement: The school has three parent-teacher conferences each year. Once a month, each division of the school (elementary, middle, high school) has a parent breakfast that is held during the school day and functions as a support group for parents.

Churchill has a very active parents association that handles the fundraising and other school events. In previous years, fundraising activities included sale of school items and holiday gifts, raffles, a book fair, and a street fair. Like many schools, the Churchill School also generates much of their fundraising through an annual spring benefit and annual appeal letter to parents and friends of the school.

Parent/Family Services: Workshops as well as social events are provided by the Churchill School throughout the school year. Of special interest is the Reading Initiative Program, which was created for 1st through 3rd graders whose families cannot afford private tutoring. The Churchill School is known for its Lecture Series, which is open to the public. The topics change on a year-by-year basis depending on the interests of parents and include well-known speakers in the field of special education. The Churchill School also provides an advisory service to assist parents in finding school placements and resources to meet their child's learning needs.

School Tours: Tours are given to parents throughout the school year. You should call the admissions office to schedule attendance at one of the Open Houses. These provide parents with the opportunity to meet staff members, hear about the school, ask questions, and tour the school.

The Application: Every child's application file is prescreened by the admissions department and/or the school psychologist or the educational director at Churchill. It's important to note that not all students who apply will be seen. An appointment will be made for a child if he/she is considered a match for an opening at the school. The admissions committee will meet to discuss your child and specifically to determine if he/she will benefit from the program and if the school has an appropriate class for your child.

The admissions staff will call you with the committee's decision concerning your child's acceptance. If the committee does not offer a place at Churchill, ask if they can suggest other possible schools for your child.

Application Fee: $50

The Clarke NYC
Auditory/Oral Center

80 East End Avenue (at 83rd Street)
New York, NY 10028
Phone (Voice/TTY): (212) 585–3500
Fax: (212) 585–3300
Head: Teresa Boemio
Web site: *www.info@clarke-nyc.org*

Grades: Kindergarten

Enrollment: 10

School Year Program: 10 Month

Summer Program: Yes

Age Range of Students: 5–7 years

School Region: 9

Funded for NYC: No

Tuition: N/A

Financial Assistance: Yes, tuition is provided by the school for those students who qualify based on the criteria for placement at Clarke.

Classifications Accepted: Deaf

Related Services: Speech Therapy, Occupational Therapy, Physical Therapy, Counseling (will provide if needed)

Student–Teacher Ratios: 10:1:1

Classroom Placement and Instruction: Clarke NYC will consider children who are deaf or hard of hearing and who need kindergarten (with an option of 2 additional years) to acquire the skills that would allow them to enter mainstream public or private schools. Their goal is to provide a nurturing environment where children can develop the auditory/oral communication skills and self-confidence that would equip them to succeed in schools with their hearing peers.

If parents are interested in applying to Clarke, it is most important that they meet the level of commitment to the auditory/oral approach that is the focus of the program. Children must have fairly good auditory skills as well as a significant delay in their communication skills to be considered for placement at the school. Most of the children considered for kindergarten will transition from Clarke's preschool program; other children would be expected to spend time in a classroom in order to be considered.

Approximately 60 to 65% of children enrolled at Clarke have cochlear implants. Currently, Clarke provides an intensive school program that focuses on all developmental domains. The emphasis is on communication skills—speech, language, and hearing. At Clarke, teachers and therapists use an auditory/oral approach with children. Speech/language services are provided every day. Unlike other schools for children who are classified as deaf or hard of hearing, Clarke does not use a total communication program; therefore, sign language is not used at the school.

All classrooms at Clarke have computers, and teachers incorporate art into classroom activities. Music is currently provided in the classroom; however, Clarke has plans to hire a music teacher. Carl Schurz Park is used for outdoor play.

Summer Program: Clarke offers a summer program that is a continuation of their school year program.

Afterschool Programs: There are no afterschool programs at Clarke at the present time.

Parent Involvement: There are no fundraising activities onsite, as the Clarke NYC school is a campus of the Clarke School for the Deaf, whose main campus is in Northampton, Massachusetts. The Development Office at the main campus handles all fundraising for all five Clarke campuses.

Parent/Family Services: There are monthly parent meetings available for all families. There is daily contact with parents through a home–school binder where notes between teachers, therapists, and parents are kept for each child at Clarke. Parents are allowed to come to Clarke anytime or can schedule an appointment to see teachers, therapists, or the director. Through parent meetings and conferences, training is provided to parents in specific techniques and strategies to benefit their children. Clarke also provides ongoing correspondence with parents through e-mail and by phone.

School Tours: Parents should contact the Head of School to discuss their child and to schedule a tour of the school.

The Application: Clarke NYC requires all evaluations, including psychological, educational, speech-language, audiological, and any other therapies (OT, PT) that your child may be receiving. A current IEP should also be included in your application.

Application Fee: None

New York Foundling Center/ John E. Coleman School

590 Avenue of the Americas
New York, NY 10011
Phone: (646) 459-3400
Fax: (646) 459-3689
Principal: Sharon Herl
Admissions: Sharon Herl
E-mail: SharonH@nyfoundling.org
Web site: *www.nyfoundling.org*

Grades: Nongraded

Enrollment: 54

School Year Program: 12 Month

Summer Program: N/A

Age Range of Students: 4–16 years

School Region: 9

Funded for NYC: Yes

Tuition: All children are funded through the CSE

Financial Assistance: Financial assistance is not applicable, since the school is housed within a hospital setting.

Classifications Accepted: Other Health Impaired (OHI), Mentally Retarded (MR), Multiple Disabilities (MD)

Related Services: Speech Therapy, Occupational Therapy, Physical Therapy, and Counseling

Student–Teacher Ratios: 6:1:2

Classroom Placement and Instruction: Since the school is based within a hospital, the teachers, therapists, and staff work very closely in working with each student individually. Due to the significant medical involvement of the children, 1:1 assistance is provided throughout the day. At times children require additional assistance for positioning, moving from one setting to another, or changes in their program. The school attempts to provide as natural a school day as possible, including music, outdoor play, and swimming through aquatic therapy as well as Reiki therapy. There is a gymnasium as well as a playground to encourage play and social skills.

Afterschool Programs: There are no afterschool programs.

Parent Involvement: There is no parent association at John E. Coleman; however, parents are encouraged to visit and participate in classroom activities whenever they can. The school has an annual Halloween parade and a fair in March.

Parent/Family Services: Parents receive training specific to their child's needs, and there is a parent/teacher conference twice a year. Training is provided during the school day and focuses on positioning and feeding, as well as how to play and interact with children who have multiple disabilities.

School Tours: Due to the medical fragility of students, parents are allowed to visit and tour the school on an individual basis. Parents should contact the principal for information.

The Application: Students are considered for placement at John E. Coleman based on referral from a CSE. Current evaluations and a current IEP are required. Since the school is in a hospital, children are provided 24-hour care and supervision along with their educational program.

Application Fee: None.

The Community School of Bergen County

11 West Forest Avenue
Teaneck, NJ 07666
Phone: (201) 837–8070
Fax: (201) 837–6799
Executive Director: Rita Rowan
Admissions: Isabel Shoukas
Web site: *www.communityschool.k12.nj.us*

Grades: K–Grade 8

School Year Program: 10 Month

Age Range of Students: 5–14 years

Funded for NYC: Yes

Financial Assistance: Yes

Enrollment: 135

Summer Program: No

School Region: Teaneck, NJ

Tuition: $27,933

Classifications Accepted: Learning Disabled (LD) and Speech Impaired (SI). The school also considers students with Attention Deficit Disorder (ADD), Attention Deficit Hyperactivity Disorder (ADHD), and perceptual impairments.

Related Services: Speech Therapy, Visual-Motor Integration and Handwriting Therapy, Guidance, and Individualized Instruction

Student–Teacher Ratios: Community has a low student-to-teacher ratio (3:1) for academic instruction.

Classroom Placement and Instruction: Students at Community are placed in homerooms based on age, but instruction is provided in homogeneous groupings. Community uses the Frostig approach to assist students with visual perceptual skills and handwriting. Community also utilizes the programs of Lindamood-Bell for instructional purposes. The school focuses on writing skills, including skills in interviewing, data collection, essays, and dialogues. The school has specialized teachers in the areas of computer, art, music, and drama. In the computer lab, students learn to use specialized programs, including PowerPoint and AlphaSmart. Music is provided once a week. The school has a gymnasium where students receive physical education every day. Health is included as part of the curriculum and is taught by a school nurse.

Enrichment is provided through social activities, field trips throughout the year, projects, and cultural experiences. Community includes dramatic performances, an art fair, and a literary magazine for students to demonstrate their unique talents.

Community has a daily behavior program for each student. Students earn points, which are exchanged for privileges. There is a time-out/crisis intervention room where children can work quietly or take time to calm themselves. Community has two psychologists on staff to assist children.

Afterschool Programs: There are no afterschool programs.

Parent Involvement: The school encourages parents to be involved in their children's education through parent–staff meetings. There is also a parents association, in which parents can participate in various school events such as luncheons, a newsletter, and an annual fashion show (the school's primary fundraiser). Community relies on parents as volunteers to assist with these activities throughout the school year.

Parent/Family Services: Community holds an Open School evening at the beginning of the school year. Parents are given numerous opportunities to meet with staff throughout the year in order to obtain information and support for their families and child. There is a series of programs in the evenings for parents, which focus on issues related to children with learning disabilities.

Community School also has outreach programs that are available to parents and professionals. These programs are presented as a series of workshops given by consultants, staff members, and specialists to provide information and strategies for working with children who have been diagnosed with learning disabilities and attention difficulties.

School Tours: Tours are given to parents and applications are accepted throughout the school year at Community. Private and public school students are considered. You should call the executive director to request information and to schedule an appointment.

The Application: Community School requires current evaluations and school records, which are reviewed prior to an initial interview with parents. Students who are considered appropriate for the program are then interviewed.

Application Fee: $50

The Martin De Porres School

136-25 218th Street
Springfield Gardens, NY 11413
Phone: (718) 525–3414
Fax: (718) 525–0982
Executive Director: Brother Raymond Blixt
Principal: John Galassi
Admissions Director: Dr. Edward Dana
Web site: *www.mdp.org*

Grades: Nongraded

Enrollment: 216

School Year Program: 10 Month

Summer Program: Yes

Age Range of Students: 7–15 years

School Region: 3

Funded for NYC: Yes

Tuition: N/A

Financial Assistance: All students receive NYCDOE funding for school

Classifications Accepted: Emotionally Disturbed (ED)

Related Services: Occupational Therapy, Physical Therapy, Speech, and Counseling

Student–Teacher Ratios: 12:1:1

Classroom Placement and Instruction: There are 17 ungraded classrooms where students are placed within an age range that does not exceed 35 months. Each classroom has three computers. Modern dance is taught 5 days a week, and classes are held in an art room once a week. Physical education is taught three times a week, and there is an indoor gymnasium as well as a playground for outdoor play. Every student attends choir class, where each child is given the opportunity to join the school chorus, which competes nationally. There is an optional culinary program. Field trips for all students occur regularly throughout the school year. There is a library with a full-time librarian.

The school has a store where students can purchase small items with behavior points they can earn. Every floor has a "behavior counselor" along with a social worker, who function to give support to a student who may need to leave the classroom at some time during the school day. These counselors stay with the student and offer brief counseling until he/she can return to the classroom. If a student needs a more extended amount of support he/she may spend approximately 20–30 minutes in a behavior room with the support of a social worker or counselor.

The Martin De Porres School has a cafeteria where the students can receive job training. There is also a fully operational café open to the students and the public, and students have the opportunity to work in the café in various capacities.

Summer Program: The Martin De Porres summer school is a 6-week program. Summer school classes mirror the academic structure, field trips, recreational, and cultural activities that the students receive throughout the school year.

Afterschool Programs: The Martin De Porres Youth Hospitality & Enrichment Center is an afterschool program offered to all students, Monday through Friday from 3:00 to 6:00 P.M. Dance, gym, and culinary classes are among the choices offered, as well as arts and crafts and a computer lab workshop for students in 5th through 12th grades. In addition, the program offers SAT preparation and homework help.

The Back to Basics Developmental League is designed for coaches to teach various sports to students of all ages.

Parent Involvement: There is no parent association at Martin De Porres at this time. Parent workshops on various subjects are conducted approximately once a month.

Parent/Family Services: The school has support groups approximately once a month on topics focusing on parenting issues, child development, and mental health issues

School Tours: Parents should call the school to schedule a tour.

The Application: Students are referred for an application through the CSE, and must have all evaluations and a current IEP.

Application Fee: None

Eagle Hill School

45 Glenville Road
Greenwich, CT 06831
Phone: (203) 622–9240
Fax: (203) 622–8668
Headmaster: Mark Griffin
Director of Admissions/Placement: Rayma-Joan Griffin
E mail: r.griffin@eaglehill.org
Web site: *www.eaglehillschool.org*

Grades: Grades 1–10   **Enrollment:** 160

School Year Program: 10 Month   **Summer Program:** Yes

Age Range of Students: 6–16 years   **School Region:** Greenwich, CT

Funded for NYC: Yes, through Emergency Interim Placement

Tuition: $40,750 day students; $52,100 residential student tuition, room, & board; $2,200 Summer program

Financial Assistance: Eagle Hill School offers assistance to qualified students. Parents must submit an application to the School and Student Service (SSS) for Financial Aid. Applications are available through the business office of the school (203–622–9240). The Financial Aid Committee meets annually to consider requests for financial assistance. Awards are based solely on need.

Classifications Accepted: Learning Disabled (LD), Speech Impaired (SI), Co-existing Learning Disabled/Attention Deficit Hyperactive Disorder (LD/ADHD)

Related Services: Speech Therapy, Occupational Therapy

Student–Teacher Ratios: Low student–teacher ratio

Classroom Placement and Instruction: Classes are nongraded at Eagle Hill. Instruction is provided through a Total Language Development approach in which children have a daily language arts tutorial, which is the core of their instructional program. While a linguistic approach is emphasized for reading and spelling, teachers also utilize multimodal, criterion-based instruction to meet the scope and sequence of skills required for learning. The low student–teacher ratio allows for a more diagnostic teaching model that focuses on the individual needs of each student.

Summer Program: The summer program at Eagle Hill is available for students ages 5 to 11 who are experiencing academic difficulty. The program is designed to immerse students in a total language environment. All students receive instruction in five academic areas, including a daily language arts tutorial. Other academic classes may include mathematics, handwriting, spelling, study skills, writing, oral language, and literature. The summer program is held Monday through Friday, from 8:00 A.M. to noon.

Afterschool Programs: Besides their core subjects, students at Eagle Hill are required to choose extracurricular activities, which are provided after 3:00 P.M. These electives provide for a wide range of interests from the arts (photography, music, drama, film) to sports (gymnastics, paddle tennis) and student clubs (yearbook, computer, student council). Additionally, Eagle Hill's interscholastic sports teams in soccer, basketball, ice and field hockey, cross-country, wrestling, volleyball, and softball participate in the Fairchester Athletic Association at three levels (grades 4, 6, and 8).

Parent Involvement: Eagle Hill has a parents association (PA) that is involved in fundraising, school events, and parent workshops at the school. Fundraising activities include the sale of school and other items, tickets for school events, a book fair and holiday boutique, and the school benefit. The PA also assists in the creation of community-building and social activities for families and students.

Parent/Family Services: Individual counseling for parents is available during the school day through advisor meetings and with the psychological support team at Eagle Hill. Support groups as well as parent workshops and training are also provided at the school during the school day and in the evening. Workshops have been presented on issues related to learning disabilities, parenting, siblings, building independence, and transition. Eagle Hill has also included guest speakers on topics related to medical issues, summer camps, and postsecondary counseling.

School Tours: Parents may visit Eagle Hill to tour the school facilities as well as to observe students and classes during the school day only after submitting an application. Applications can be obtained by calling the admissions office.

The Application: A current psychoeducational evaluation, school reports, and any specialists' reports as well as work samples in writing and math must be submitted to Eagle Hill as part of your child's file. A school release-of-information form must also be completed. This information along with the parents' interview is required prior to your child being considered for a possible placement at the school.

A student visit may be scheduled by contacting the school's office only after his/her file is complete. Students who are invited to visit the school attend classes with a student host. They will also join the student host for lunch and will meet with the director of admissions during their visit. Students are accepted to Eagle Hill School on a rolling admissions basis. Parents are notified of the admission decision within a week of their child's visit to the school.

Application Fee: $50

The Gateway School

236 Second Avenue
New York, NY 10003
Phone: (212) 777–5966
Fax: (212) 777–5794
Executive Director: Robert Cunningham
Admissions Director: Sharyn Lico
Web site: *www.gatewayschool.org*

Grades: Nongraded

School Year Program: 10 Month

Age Range of Students: 5–12 years

Funded for NYC: Yes

Enrollment: 62

Summer Program: No

School Region: 9

Tuition: $34,500

Financial Assistance: Parents apply to the School and Student Service (SSS) for Financial Aid. Eligibility and amount available are determined on an annual basis by the Gateway School's Board of Trustees.

Classifications Accepted: Learning Disabled (LD), Speech Impaired (SI), Other Health Impaired (OHI)

Related Services: Occupational Therapy, Speech/Language Therapy, and Counseling

Student–Teacher Ratios: 8:1:1 for Lower School (5–10 years old), 10:1:1 for Transition Program

Classroom Placement and Instruction: Classes at Gateway are formed based on a student's cognitive, academic, and social skill levels. The Lower School program is highly individualized and structured for students ages 5 through 9. Math and reading groups are formed across classes according to each student's ability. In addition, one-to-one instruction is available through the remedial specialist. The school uses a combination of reading programs including Orton-Gillingham and the Wilson Reading System. Math is taught using the Stern Structural Arithmetic Program. Cursive writing is taught at the youngest age level to promote handwriting fluency; a student may receive group or individual support by the occupational therapist or remedial specialist. Social studies and science are often integrated into other areas of the curriculum, and the students go on frequent field trips during the school year. Lower School students have adaptive physical education in the school's gymnasium for 30 minutes every morning.

Students in the Transition Program are age 9½ to 12. The curriculum follows the New York State Learning Standards, modified toward students' individual needs. Health education is also taught at this age level. Students receive instruction in soccer, basketball, volleyball, and floor hockey. An important element of the Transition Program is the weekly meeting, which is geared to help students prepare for graduating from the school as well as to understand their individual learning styles.

All Gateway students are taught computer skills, the youngest individually. Each classroom has a computer station, and there is a computer lab. The school has a library, roof terrace playground, occupational therapy floor, and science and art facilities. Part of the Gateway School's social development program is the Lower School assembly, which is held 4 days a week in their Grandstand room/communal space. This allows the students to practice their listening, attending, and presenting skills as a group, in a nurturing environment.

Afterschool Programs: Afterschool activities change each trimester. Activities in the past have included cooking, drama, dance, and chess. The school has an afterschool exchange program with Friends Seminary, located one block away.

Parent Involvement: Gateway has a parent association as well as individual class representatives. Once a month a parent from each class reads a story to their child's class in the library. Parents participate in school activities such as the book fair, holiday party, and fundraising events.

Parent/Family Services: Gateway provides a series of meetings in the evenings to assist parents with transitioning to the school. Parent conferences are held three times a year; however, parents can request additional conferences as needed. Gateway also offers workshops throughout the school year on topics of interest to parents. These are provided free of charge to all Gateway parents.

School Tours: Tours of Gateway are scheduled twice a month, beginning in October. The tours give parents the opportunity to spend a morning at the school, where they can observe the program, hear presentations, and ask questions. At the end of a visit, parents can schedule an individual conference with one of the school's psychologists or the director of admissions.

The Application: Parents can request an application by phoning the school or can receive an application when they visit the school. A completed application includes a current (within 18 months) psycho-educational evaluation, current reports from professionals who have been currently working with your child, recent school reports, and a signed release form. It will expedite your child's application and consideration for placement at Gateway if you submit all evaluations and reports along with the application.

Admissions Process: If, after receiving an application, the admissions committee feels that the school might be appropriate for a child, an appointment is scheduled for him/her to be evaluated. Once Gateway completes their evaluation, they will meet with you and provide feedback regarding their findings. If they do not feel that your child would be appropriate for their program, they will recommend other programs to you. Gateway uses a rolling admissions policy.

Application Fee: $85

The Stephen Gaynor School

22 West 74th Street
New York, NY 10023
(New Address as of Sept. 2006:
174 West 90th Street, New York, NY 10024)
Phone: (212) 787–7070
Fax: (212) 787–3312
Head: Dr. Scott Gaynor
Admissions: Jackie Long
E-mail: info@sgaynor.com
Web site: *www.sgaynor.com*

Grades: Nongraded

Enrollment: 122 (As of 9/06, 165)

School Year Program: 10 Month

Summer Program: No

Age Range of Students: 5–14 years

School Region: 10

Funded for NYC: Yes

Tuition: $34,650

Financial Assistance: Yes, based on financial need of student and family

Classifications Accepted: Learning Disabled (LD)

Related Services: Speech Therapy, Occupational Therapy, Physical Therapy

Student–Teacher Ratios: 8–10 students with 1 teacher and 1 assistant teacher

Classroom Placement and Instruction: Stephen Gaynor has 1 or 2 classes for each age range, with student groups being within 1 year of their chronological age. There is one head teacher and one assistant for each class of 8 to 10 students. While using primarily a multisensory language-based approach to teaching, Stephen Gaynor also uses a variety of curricula and programs within each content area to meet student needs. These include:

- Reading: Orton-Gillingham Phonics
- Math: Stern Structural Mathematics materials and other manipulative aids
- Handwriting: Handwriting Without Tears

Science and social studies are taught using a sequential skills-based curriculum that includes multisensory, hands-on experiences. Art, music, and adapted physical education are provided through developmentally age-appropriate lessons and activities. The arts program at Stephen Gaynor includes fine arts, crafts, and drama.

Afterschool Programs: Stephen Gaynor provides a wide range of afterschool activities for children. These include tutoring, art, music, gym, computer, photography, and chess.

Parent Involvement: The parent association holds monthly meetings and handles a full calendar of events for the school year. There are several fundraising events as well as social events such as a sports night and dinner, and Chelsea Piers day. The PTA plans events throughout the school year in which parents can participate. The Lecture Series presented at Stephen Gaynor is created through suggestions made by the PTA to the Head of the School.

One of the PTA's efforts is publishing *The Gaynor Gazette,* which features information on staff and alums, special events at the school, and spotlights on classroom learning. Fundraising activities include the sale of school items and holiday items, raffles, the annual school benefit, and an annual appeal letter.

Parent/Family Services: Stephen Gaynor has a parent lecture series each year that is provided free-of-charge through the PTA. The lecture series has presented several well-known speakers in the field of education, such as Dr. Robert Brooks, Dr. Mel Levine, and Dr. Stanley Turecki. In the past, workshops have featured topics on ADD and ADHD, medications, social skills, sex education, parenting, homework, and understanding learning disabilities.

School Tours: Tours of Stephen Gaynor are conducted individually through the admissions office. Parents should call the admissions director for information and to schedule a visit to the school.

The Application: Any child applying to Stephen Gaynor must have a psychoeducational evaluation to be considered for placement. If a child is considered a possible candidate for the school, then the child is asked to come to the school for an academic evaluation by the admissions team. If the team is unsure as to whether a child is appropriate, they will have the child spend time in one of the classes at Stephen Gaynor. Parents will be given feedback within 1 week of the child's evaluation by the admissions team.

Application Fee: $150 (includes academic evaluation)

The Gillen Brewer School

410 East 92nd Street
New York, NY 10128
Phone: (212) 831–3667
Fax: (212) 831–5254
Head of School: Donna Kennedy
Assistant Head of School: Milt Sleeter
E-mail: donna@gillenbrewer.com
Web site: *www.gillenbrewer.com*

Grades: Nongraded

Enrollment: 84

School Year Program: 10 or 12 Month

Summer Program: Yes

Age Range of Students: 2.7–10 years

School Region: 9

Funded for NYC: Yes

Tuition: $45,000

Financial Assistance: No

Classifications Accepted: Learning Disabled (LD), Emotionally Disturbed (ED), Speech Impaired (SI), Other Health Impaired (OHI)

Related Services: Occupational Therapy, Speech Therapy, and Counseling

Student–Teacher Ratios: 8:1:1 and 10:1:1

Classroom Placement and Instruction: Currently the school has three preschool classes and six school-age classes. While Gillen Brewer follows the New York State Learning Standards, teachers provide individualized learning to meet each student's specific needs. Reading and writing are taught through a balanced literacy program and a multisensory phonetically based approach. Math is taught through a hands-on approach using manipulatives and visuals. Science and social studies focus on developmentally appropriate topics based on the New York State Learning Standards.

Gillen Brewer has strong art and music programs. The art program, which includes fine arts and crafts, is provided through an art therapist. The music program is taught by a music teacher trained in Kodaly. Both art and music are provided three times a week. Drama and yoga are also incorporated into the school program. Children at Gillen

Brewer are given opportunities to participate in many of New York City's cultural events through museum and theater trips.

Gillen Brewer has a computer lab, gymnasium, and roof terrace, as well as two sensory gyms for occupational therapy. The school can take a child for either a 10-month or a 12-month program. Swimming, during the summer program at a nearby pool, is available at an additional cost.

Summer Program: The Gillen Brewer School has a 6-week summer school program that is a continuation of the school year's curriculum. In addition, the students go on various field trips and participate in community-oriented activities. Swimming is provided two times a week during the summer through "Take Me to the Water," a program that provides transportation to local pools as well as swimming instruction.

Afterschool Programs: Gillen Brewer provides afterschool tutoring.

Parent Involvement: The parent association is instrumental in planning school events. They offer support to incoming families through a New Parent Orientation and New Parent Phase-in newsletter. The Gillen Brewer parent association is actively involved in fundraising activities such a sale of school items and gift-wrap, a book fair, and an annual spring benefit. Gillen Brewer also has a grandparents/family association.

Parent/Family Services: Parent support groups take place during the school day, and individual counseling for parents is offered at that time as well. Workshops for parents are offered both during the day and in the evening. The following topics have been included in previous workshops: play, speech, OT, problem-solving, nutrition (S.A.N.E.), handwriting, transitions, medications, and playdates.

School Tours: Gillen Brewer has monthly tours beginning in the fall of each school year. Parents should contact the assistant head to schedule a tour. Applications can be obtained by calling the school.

The Application: A neuropsychological or psychoeducational evaluation, current educational and classroom reports, and an IEP are required for consideration for placement at Gillen Brewer. After an initial screening, children who are considered appropriate for the program will be scheduled for a full-day class visit. Parents are notified by phone regarding acceptance at the school within 2 weeks.

Application Fee: None

The Hallen School

97 Centre Avenue
New Rochelle, NY 10801
Phone: (914) 636–6600
Fax: (914) 633–4089
Executive Director: Carol LoCascio, Ph. D.
Principal of Lower School: Stephanie Dalbey
Dean of Admissions: James Welker
Web site: *www.hallenschool.com*

Grades: K–Grade 12

School Year Program: 10 Month

Age Range of Students: 5–21 years

Funded for NYC: Yes

Financial Assistance: Yes

Enrollment: 120

Summer Program: Yes

School Region: New Rochelle, NY

Tuition: $28,000 (10 months)

Classifications Accepted: Speech Impaired (SI), Learning Disabled (LD), Emotionally Disturbed (ED), Other Health Impaired (OHI), Autistic (AUT)

Related Services: Speech Therapy, Occupational Therapy, Counseling, and Art Therapy

Student–Teacher Ratios: 6:1:1, 6:1:2, 12:1:1, 12:1:2

Classroom Placement and Instruction: The Hallen School is divided into a Lower School (K–Grade 6), a Middle School (Grades 7–8), and an Upper School (Grades 9–12). Classes are graded, with a possible 3-year age range in each classroom. The school follows the New York State Learning Standards to develop curriculum. Hallen has a small library, but classes also use the New Rochelle library nearby. The school has a computer room, gymnasium, and sensory gyms. They also lease an outdoor space at a local Catholic school nearby. A fine arts program and a music program are provided through a separate art room. There is also a gardening program, which is run by the art teacher. Children eat in their classrooms. Students can bring their own lunch or purchase food at a café at the school.

The Lower and Middle Schools at Hallen have self-contained classes in which individualized instruction can be provided to each student. The Lower School classes have six students with a special education teacher and either one or two assistant teachers. The Middle School also has self-contained small classes, but with higher student–teacher ratios. Every student has a schedule, which is individualized by a color assigned to each child. The schedule utilizes icons on a chart, which can be checked off when activities are completed. Independent work is also assigned. The Lower School uses the TEACCH method for learning, a program designed through the University of North Carolina. All teachers use TEACCH and receive ongoing training throughout the school year. Each classroom has its own behavior system.

In the Upper School, Hallen provides a high school curriculum through which students may obtain a Regents, local, or IEP diploma.

Reading is provided through a range of programs, including Orton-Gillingham, Wilson, and Edmark, and uses chapter books to develop comprehension. Math utilizes several programs and is individualized based upon a student's abilities. Hallen uses Social Stories as developed by Carol Gray, and games are included for further socialization skills.

Summer Program: Hallen has a summer program to maintain academic skills and therapy mandates for students. A focus of the summer program is a science project in which students participate in water-related activities at a nearby center. The summer program also includes more outdoor activities and field trips for students.

Afterschool Programs: There are no afterschool programs, as the majority of students have to travel a long distance from their homes to the school.

Parent Involvement: Due to the location of the school and the fact that most of their students are transported to New Rochelle from New York City, there is no parent association at Hallen. However, parents are encouraged to be involved in their child's educational program, and individual parent counseling is provided upon request. Hallen has a consulting psychiatrist twice a week, and 13 social workers to assist students and their families.

Since the school is a for-profit institution, there is no fundraising required of parents.

Parent/Family Services: Every student has a therapist for counseling who is available to parents during the school day. Some workshops and parent training are provided to coordinate school and home programs such as TEACCH. The school attempts to make workshops and training specific to child and home needs.

School Tours: Parents will be called to tour Hallen only if the admissions committee feels that the child might be appropriate for the program.

The Application: The application for Hallen begins with a packet from the CSE, which includes all evaluations and a current IEP. Parents accompany their child to the school, where the student is expected to go into a classroom to visit as long as he/she can tolerate. If a student is having difficulty in spending time in the classroom, Hallen allows students to return several times to visit in order to help them in determining whether they can meet a child's needs as well as his/her IEP recommendations. Hallen will then send a letter to the parent indicating whether the school can provide a placement for the child.

Application Fee: None

Hebrew Academy for Special Education (HASC)

6220 14th Avenue
Brooklyn, NY 11219
Phone: (718) 331–1624
Fax: (718) 331–9403
Program Director: Debra Mandel
Director of Operations: Jeanne Alter
E-mail: cs.mandel@hasc.net
Web site: *www.hasc.net*

Grades: Nongraded

Enrollment: 76

School Year Program: 12 months

Summer Program: Yes

Age Range of Students: 5–21 years

School Region: 7

Funded for NYC: Yes

Tuition: All tuition is received from funding for children through CSE

Financial Assistance: N/A

Classifications Accepted: Other Health Impaired (OHI), Mentally Retarded (MR), Multiple Disabilities (MD)

Related Services: HASC has two Occupational Therapy and Physical Therapy rooms. Speech and Language Therapy are provided both in and outside the classroom.

Student–Teacher Ratios: The school has a range of staff-per-child ratios, including 6:1:2, 8:1:2, 12:1:4, 12:1:2, and 12:1:1. Medically fragile children are placed in a classroom of 6:1:2 along with a nurse.

Classroom Placement and Instruction: There are 10 classes in which the children are grouped according to age as well as cognitive ability. The school's intention is to teach functioning skills as they apply to daily living, as well as academics and social functioning skills. HASC provides musical therapy, psychological services, and some classrooms contain adaptive computers. In addition, HASC developed a program called Teaching and Educating Autistic Children with Multi Modalities (TEAMM) for children with pervasive developmental delays and/ or Autism.

The lunchroom, which provides daily kosher breakfast and lunch, also functions as an entertainment room where the children watch a performance or engage in an interactive activity provided by different organizations. There is an outdoor play area with adaptive equipment, as well as an accessible bathroom.

An important part of the program is adaptive living, and at the age of approximately 14 years the school begins transition services and prevocational training. There is a prevocational room that has a washing machine and dryer, a soda machine, and a copier machine, all of which the students learn to independently operate. Students at the same age participate in a travel training program in order to better assist and prepare them for independent travel. There are two nurses at the school.

Summer Program: Camp HASC is located in the Catskill Mountains in upstate New York and is a sleepaway camp that maintains the educational and therapeutic services for children as well as a full range of recreational summer camp activities.

Afterschool Programs: There is an afterschool recreational program for teenagers that is nonacademic and intended for socialization.

Parent Involvement: There is no parent association at this time.

Parent/Family Services: Individual counseling is available for parents, as well as evening workshops.

School Tours: Parents should contact the school for a tour.

The Application: Application to HASC is initiated through a referral from the CSE. The school must receive a child's packet, including current evaluations and a current IEP, from the NYCDOE in order to consider a child for placement. HASC accepts outside evaluations as well as conducts their own testing. This is provided at no cost to families of children with suspected delays in cognitive ability, living and self-help skills, and fine and gross motor development as well as other areas of delay. Certified bilingual staff members can conduct evaluations in English, Hebrew, Russian, Spanish, and Yiddish. HASC will meet independently with a child and family for admissions. Occasionally, a child will visit a class in order for staff to observe his/her skills and ability to interact with other children.

Application Fee: None

The Lavelle School for the Blind and Visually Impaired

3830 Paulding Avenue
Bronx, NY 10469
Phone: (718) 882–1212
Fax: (718) 882–0005
Superintendent: Frank Simpson
Intake Coordinator: Awilda Bravo
E-mail: fsimpson@lavelleschool.org
Web site: *www.lavelleschool.org*

Grades: Pre-K–Grade 12

Enrollment: 108

School Year Program: 10 Month

Summer Program: Yes

Age Range of Students: 3–21 years

School Region: 2

Funded for NYC: Yes

Tuition: All students at Lavelle are funded through the NYCDOE

Financial Assistance: N/A

Classifications Accepted: Blind, Multiple Disabilities (MD)

Related Services: Speech Therapy, Occupational Therapy, Physical Therapy, Orientation and Mobility Training, Counseling, Nursing

Student–Teacher Ratios: 6:1:2, 6:1:1, 12:1:4

Classroom Placement and Instruction: There are 23 classes at Lavelle, including preschool. Classrooms are ungraded. Due to the significant disabilities of their students, Lavelle has more therapists than teachers. They also have bilingual teachers, nurses, and social workers. The emphasis at Lavelle is on providing maximum support for students to achieve their potential. The daily focus is on developing a personal communication system for every student so that he/she can be independent. Communication systems may include gestures, symbols, speech, Braille, and augmentative communication devices. Every classroom has two computers for students to learn beginning literacy skills and keyboarding skills. Instruction is also provided in daily living skills, with the emphasis on transferring skills to the student's home.

Summer Program: Lavelle has a summer program that is a continuation of academic instruction and therapy mandates.

Afterschool Programs: Lavelle's afterschool program was created in association with the Office of Mental Retardation and Developmental Disabilities (OMRDD). Thirty students participate in a music band in afterschool.

Parent Involvement: While there is no formal parent association at Lavelle, parents do come together about specific issues such as parenting classes, transitions, and advocacy.

Parent/Family Services: Parent workshops at Lavelle are scheduled to help parents and families find community resources to assist them with medical, mental health, or other issues related to their child and family.

School Tours: Students are considered for placement at Lavelle through a referral from the CSE, based upon their classification as Blind or Multiply Disabled. Parents should contact the intake coordinator to schedule a tour for themselves as well as an interview for their child.

The Application: Children are referred to Lavelle School through the CSE process. Current evaluations and a current IEP are required to be considered for the school.

Application Fee: None

The League School

567 Kingston Avenue
Brooklyn, NY 11203
Phone: (718) 498–2500
Fax: (718) 778–4018
Principal: Stephanie Golub

Grades: Nongraded

School Year Program: 10 Month

Age Range of Students: 5–12 years

Funded for NYC: Yes

Financial Assistance: N/A

Enrollment: 135

Summer Program: No

School Region: 17

Tuition: N/A

Classifications Accepted: Emotionally Disturbed (ED), Autistic (AUT), Asperger's Syndrome (AS)

Related Services: Occupational Therapy, Physical Therapy, Speech, Counseling, and Applied Behavior Analysis

Student–Teacher Ratios: 8:1:1, 6:1:1, 12:1:1

Classroom Placement and Instruction: The curriculum at the League School follows the New York State Learning Standards and includes reading (including remedial reading), computer, art, music, theater arts, science, social studies, mathematics, and adaptive physical education. Older students attend prevocational training classes. There is a large staff-to-student ratio at the League School. The school uses several types of therapeutic behavioral systems within the classroom and as a reward system for students to earn various privileges. The school has a games room, an outside playground, a music room, and an art room. There is an annual science fair at the school, as well as a school talent show and harvest festival. A school café run by the Department of Education is on the premises and serves breakfast and lunch.

Afterschool Programs: The League School does not have an afterschool program.

Parent Involvement: There is a parent association at the League School.

Parent/Family Services: Each family is assigned a "personal treatment cocoordinator" to monitor the progress of their child.

School Tours: Parents should call the school to schedule a tour.

The Application: The League School receives referrals through the CBST. The application must include current evaluations and an IEP.

Application Fee: None

LearningSpring Elementary School

254 West 29th Street, 4th Floor
New York, NY 10001
Phone: (212) 239–4926
Fax: (212) 239–5226
Head: Margaret Poggi
Admissions: Margaret Poggi
E-mail: Director@learningspring.org
Web site: *www.learningspring.org*

Grades: Nongraded

School Year Program: 10 Month

Age Range of Students: 5–12 years

Funded for NYC: Yes

Financial Assistance: No

Enrollment: 56

Summer Program: Yes

School Region: 9

Tuition: $27,000

Classifications Accepted: Speech Impaired (SI), Learning Disabled (LD), Emotionally Disturbed (ED), Other Health Impaired (OHI), Autistic (AUT)

Related Services: Speech Therapy, Occupational Therapy, and Counseling

Student–Teacher Ratios: 8:1:2

Classroom Placement and Instruction: Students are placed in classrooms based on their language and social skills within a 3-year age range (6–8, 8–10, 9–11, 10–12 years). LearningSpring uses the New York State Learning Standards as well as other programs to develop the curriculum. Preventing Academic Failure is used for teaching reading and handwriting skills. LearningSpring also includes Balanced Literacy in their reading program. Math instruction is presented through a hands-on approach. Reading and math groups are created across classrooms. Social studies and science are introduced through themes that are extended throughout the school year.

The school has a library and a movement room for students. Each class has library time once a week. Children bring their lunch to school, and classes combine for lunch and recess to expand socialization skills. Art is presented through class projects; however, there is an art teacher who works with each class once a week. Music and drama are both provided in the movement room at the school, which also serves as the lunchroom. LearningSpring includes yoga as part of the adaptive physical education program, and classes use several neighborhood playgrounds for outdoor play.

LearningSpring uses a variety of interventions to improve students' pragmatic language and social skills development, including Relationship Development Intervention (RDI), Social Stories, Cognitive-Behavioral Therapy, and Role Playing.

Summer Program: LearningSpring provides a 6-week summer program for those students with a 12-month mandate on their IEP. The program encourages social skills and learning in an academic environment with practice provided through community activities. Swimming and weekly field trips are also included during the summer program.

Afterschool Programs: The afterschool program at LearningSpring was developed by the adaptive physical education teacher, who coordinates various activities depending on the interests of the students each semester.

Parent Involvement: LearningSpring has an active parent association, which handles fundraising and school events as well as parent workshops. School fundraising activities include an annual book fair to benefit the school library and classrooms as well as sales of candy, holiday, and gift items throughout the year. As with most New York City schools, the parent association's major fundraising event is a spring benefit.

Parent/Family Services: LearningSpring has parent meetings every week where the parents meet with different school professionals and can view videos of their children. Parent meetings are held on a rotating basis according to class, with each class of parents meeting approximately six to seven times within a school year. LearningSpring provides individual counseling for parents and is starting support groups as well. Individual counseling is available both during the school day and in the evening. Support groups are presented in the evenings on a monthly basis and often include guest speakers.

School Tours: School tours at LearningSpring are held twice a year, in September and January. Parents should call the school to schedule a tour.

The Application: Parents can receive an application by calling LearningSpring. Applications should include current evaluations including psychoeducational, speech and language, occupational therapy, and psychiatric (with a diagnosis), as well as a current IEP. The completed application will be reviewed by the admissions team. If a student is considered a possible candidate for admission, LearningSpring will schedule a visit for the child to the school, which lasts approximately a half-day.

Application Fee: $50

The Lorge School

353 West 17th St.
New York, NY 10011
Phone: (212) 929–8660
Fax: (212) 989–8249
Executive Director: Michael Pagliuca
Clinical Supervisor & Intake Coordinator:
Deborah Kasner

Grades: K–Grade 12

Enrollment: 105

School Year Program: 10 Month

Summer Program: Yes

Age Range of Students: 5–18 years

School Region: 9

Funded for NYC: Yes

Tuition: $21,553

Financial Assistance: N/A

Classifications Accepted: Learning Disabled (LD), Emotionally Disturbed (ED)

Related Services: Occupational Therapy, Speech Therapy, and Counseling

Student–Teacher Ratios: 8:1:1 in the lower school and 12:1:1 in the middle and upper schools

Classroom Placement and Instruction: Children are placed in classes according to age and ability within a 36-month range. The overall goal and intent of the Lorge School is to provide an academic environment that nurtures and supports children who are primarily emotionally disturbed or learning disabled. The reading program is phonetic-based; they use the Orton-Gillingham reading program. The Junior Great Book Series is used for language arts.

The Lorge School uses a program designed to reinforce social skills and on-task behavior. The school implements a daily "Points Sheet" that monitors successful behavioral goals for each student. Goals are monitored four times each class period, and point sheets are totaled and sent home. Earned points are used for special school activities. Crisis interventionists help students throughout the school day for long- and short-term time-outs from their classrooms.

The school has a computer room, library, gymnasium, cafeteria, art room, and music room. On Friday afternoons there is an arts enrichment program that includes playwriting, drumming, and dance. Students can compete in the nonpublic-school basketball league. Students in the upper school participate in a vocational training program.

Summer Program: The Lorge School has a 6-week summer program for those students whoes IEPs mandate 12-month services. The focus of the program is on basic skills and community-based activities. The purpose of the summer program is to maintain academic progress from the school year. In addition, students go on field trips and go swimming in local facilities.

Afterschool Programs: The school offers a social skills group as an afterschool program.

Parent Involvement: Parent–staff conferences are held twice a year, with additional informal meetings throughout the year specific to each child.

School Tours: Parents should call the school for a tour.

The Application: Parents should call for an application, or they may complete the application at an intake appointment. An applicant will be observed in a classroom setting at the Lorge School, as part of the intake appointment. Current evaluations and an IEP are required for the application to Lorge.

Application Fee: None

The Lowell School

203-05 32nd Avenue
Bayside, NY 11361
Phone: (718) 352–2100; (718) 352–2156
Fax: (718) 352–3654
Executive Director: Dede Proujansky
Principal: Susan Price
Clinical Coordinator: Ruth Joseph
E-mail: tlschool@aol.com
Web site: *www.thelowellschool.com*

Grades: Grades 3–8

School Year Program: 10 Month

Age Range of Students: 8–14 years

Funded for NYC: Yes

Financial Assistance: N/A

Enrollment: 110

Summer Program: Yes

School Region: 3

Tuition: $24,000

Classifications Accepted: Speech Impaired (SI), Learning Disabled (LD), Emotionally Disturbed (ED), Other Health Impaired (OHI)

Related Services: Speech Therapy, Occupational Therapy, Physical Therapy, Counseling

Student–Teacher Ratios: 12:1:1

Classroom Placement and Instruction: Most classes have a 2-year age range at Lowell. There is one class for each of the lower grades (3rd through 5th) and two classes for each of the older grades (6th through 8th). Students are expected to move independently between classes.

The Lowell School follows the New York State Learning Standards. Within specific content areas, the school uses a variety of curricula. The reading curriculum includes Orton-Gillingham and literature-based reading. Students receive 1:1 reading instruction twice a week for 45 minutes. Handwriting Without Tears is used for handwriting development. Students are expected to write a book report each month. Modified materials are used for science and social studies, providing hands-on, experiential activities in each subject. The arts program at

Lowell is taught once a week by an art therapist who incorporates a range of fine arts (drawing, painting, crafts, etc.) into the program. The students also receive music once a week. The Lowell Choir has made a CD every year since 2002.

Lowell has a computer center that serves all classrooms. Students are required to do 10 minutes of keyboard skills each day. The computer teacher uses a range of computer programs (i.e., Read Write and Type, Easy Books) to assist students in maximizing computers for learning. Third through 5th graders have one period of computer on a weekly basis; upper grades have double periods once a week. Students in grades 6 through 8 use computers for special assignments such as book reports and spreadsheets. Students are also instructed in the use of PowerPoint and Print Shop in the computer center.

There are a range of student activities at Lowell, including the Honor Society, reading clubs, student volunteer program, and student government. The student government, comprised of 7th- and 8th-grade students, meets bimonthly and is responsible for a variety of activities for the students.

A daily behavior program has been established at Lowell that relates to student work ethic, respect for others, and a target behavior specific to each individual student. Students carry daily point sheets from class to class, which can be redeemed for privileges each week. Students must earn 90% of points in order to participate in certain activities. Privileges may include extra gym time, computer games, bakery, movies, and school trips.

Lowell's facilities include a computer room, library and media center, gymnasium, playground, garden, art room, and multipurpose room, which is used for assemblies and special school events and is also utilized for remedial tutoring. There is an outdoor area where students may eat and socialize under the supervision by Lowell staff.

Summer Program: Lowell School has a 6-week summer program. Instruction is focused on a central theme which culminates in a fair at the end of the summer. There are weekly field trips and students have gym and computer classes daily.

Afterschool Programs: Lowell does not have afterschool programs.

Parent Involvement: Lowell has a parent association that is very involved in fundraising and school events. Fundraising activities include a walkathon, sale of school and gift items, tickets for school events, raffles, and lunch sales. A spring benefit auction ("Love for Lowell") is held annually for families and friends. Lowell has an end-of-year dinner dance that is attended by both parents and students. At this event, every child is given some type of recognition for his/her efforts and achievements.

There is a school newspaper that is printed every month for parents that updates them about school events and classroom news.

Parent/Family Services: Ms. Price, the principal of Lowell, explained that since students come from all boroughs of New York, it is often difficult to arrange workshops or support groups to meet every family's needs. However, Lowell does work with families to assist them with advocacy and educational resources. Individual counseling is available for parents at the school.

School Tours: Lowell has two open houses each year, usually in November and January. You should call the clinical coordinator to schedule attendance at an open house. At this time, parents will have the opportunity to meet staff members, hear about the school, ask questions, and tour Lowell. Parents meet with the principal and clinical coordinator individually at a later date after completing the application.

The Application: Lowell requires the following information to be complete in order to consider a child for admission: application, release form, educational evaluation, social history, psychological testing (within 2 years), current IEP, and a teacher report form. A child's packet is screened by an admissions team, and an intake interview is scheduled if there is a placement. Both the student and parent attend the interview. The clinical coordinator will contact you regarding the admissions decision for your child.

Application Fee: $50 nonrefundable (nonfunded applicants only)

The McCarton School

350 East 82nd Street
New York, NY 10028
Phone: (212) 996–9019
Fax: (212) 996–9047
Executive Director: Dr. Cecilia McCarton
Educational Director: Dr. Ivy Feldman
Associate Educational Director: Jackie Hickey
Web site: *www.mccartonschool.org*

Grades: Nongraded

Enrollment: 22

School Year Program: 12 Month

Summer Program: Yes

Age Range of Students: 3–9 years

School Region: 9

Funded for NYC: No

Tuition: $70,000 per year

Financial Assistance: A scholarship fund provides financial assistance for families who are unable to obtain an education for their child.

Classifications Accepted: Autism (AUT)

Related Services: Speech Therapy, Physical Therapy

Student–Teacher Ratios: 1:1

Classroom Placement and Instruction: The school provides 1:1 educational intervention for children who are diagnosed with Autism. Children are placed in classrooms based on their cognitive and language abilities. Applied Behavior Analysis (ABA) is primarily used in the classrooms. Verbal behavior and natural environmental teaching are also used at the school.

An individualized curriculum is written for each child by the educational director and associate educational director. The speech therapist writes and implements the language curriculum for the classroom. The head teacher then supervises the ABA trainers who are responsible for following the child's curricula each day. Speech therapists and occupational therapists spend at least 1 hour each day in the classroom. Sensory integration strategies are provided by the OT within the classroom.

Facilities at the McCarton School include a library, gymnasium, cafeteria, and art area. The art program includes fine arts (drawing, painting, etc.) and music twice a week. Computers are available in every classroom. The school rents playground space at St. Stephen of Hungary on East 82nd Street for outdoor activities. The students also take swimming lessons once a week at a private pool on the Upper East Side.

Summer Program: The school has a 6-week summer day camp to provide opportunities for the children to develop their play and social skills. Students have adaptive physical education and swimming four times a week and have a field trip scheduled one day a week.

Afterschool Programs: There are no afterschool programs at the McCarton School; however, some children can receive additional therapy for an additional cost after school. Many of the students go to afterschool activities within the community.

Parent Involvement: The McCarton School has a PTA that is very involved in fundraising, school events, and parent workshops. The annual school benefit and a comedy night are the primary means for fundraising. Parents also participate in a speaker series to address a range of relevant topics for families of children with Autism, including research, education, and intervention.

Parent/Family Services: Every child at the McCarton School has a home-school staff member, usually a teacher, who coordinates with the family on the child's individualized program. This assures that everyone is using the same intervention and implementing the program consistently.

As part of each child's program, parents are provided individual counseling 2 hours each week to work with either the educational director or the associate educational director. A social worker also provides parent support groups twice a month in the evenings. Once a month, the teachers at McCarton participate in a sibling group, which is supervised by a clinical psychologist, and provides opportunities for children and siblings to socialize.

Viewing booths with one-way mirrors are also available for parents to observe their child without disrupting the routine of the classroom. Parents do not have to make a request to observe their child—they are allowed to do so at any time.

Communication with parents is very personal at the McCarton School. Parents usually drop off and pick up their children each day, and have time to speak to teachers and staff at those times. Additionally, daily notebooks and a weekly newsletter are sent home. E-mail is also utilized for all classes.

School Tours: Tours are given to parents throughout the school year. Parents should call the educational director for a tour and application.

The Application: A diagnosis of Autism or Autism Spectrum Disorder is required for applying to the McCarton School. There is a three-page application that must be completed initially. After reviewing the application, the school will request more information from parents when a placement becomes available. If a child fits the profile for the McCarton School, an observation will be scheduled at his/her current school. The child will be asked to visit the McCarton School for an intake appointment only if there is an opening.

Application Fee: None

The Mary McDowell Center for Learning

20 Bergen Street
Brooklyn, NY 11201
Phone: (718) 625–3939
Fax: (718) 625–1456
Head of School: Debbie Zlotowitz
Assistant Head: Beth Schneider
Admissions Director: Deborah Edel
E-mail: info@mmcl.net
Web site: *www.marymcdowell.org*

Grades: Nongraded

Enrollment: 151

School Year Program: 10 Month

Summer Program: Yes

Age Range of Students: 5–14 years

School Region: 15

Funded for NYC: No

Tuition: $31,975—Elementary School; $33,975—Middle School

Financial Assistance: Yes, as determined by the School and Student Service (SSS) for Financial Aid. The package is returned to the school from SSS for review.

Classifications Accepted: Learning Disabled (LD)

Related Services: Occupational Therapy, Speech and Language Therapy, and Counseling

Student–Teacher Ratios: 12:1:1

Classroom Placement and Instruction: Mary McDowell Center for Learning is divided into the Elementary Division, the Upper Elementary Division, and the Middle School classes known as houses. Classes at the school are grouped within a 36-month age range; the youngest children generally have eight or nine students in their classroom. Language arts, math, and social studies are taught within the classroom. Students are regrouped for reading with children from other classes according to ability. Programs used for reading include Preventing Academic Failure (PAF) and Alphabetic Phonics.

The writing program includes Handwriting PAF (Preventing Academic Failure), Scientific Spelling, and Spellwell. Teachers use adaptations, and a wide variety of materials and resources are used to accommodate students based on their individual needs. Listening and speaking skills are taught within the context of the classroom as well as in group speech therapy sessions. The resources used in the mathematics curriculum include Marilyn Burns Replacement Units, Attack Math, and Stern Structural Arithmetic, as well as other programs and materials. In addition to math lessons that include the whole class, students are assessed by their teachers and placed into smaller individualized groups within the classroom based on their ability levels.

The Mary McDowell Center for Learning has a science lab with two science teachers, a computer lab with a computer teacher, a library with a full-time librarian, and a gymnasium. The students bring their own lunch to school and eat with their classrooms in the school cafeteria. Students in the Upper Elementary Division go once a week, with their teachers, to one of many of the neighborhood restaurants at lunchtime and bring their purchased lunches back to eat in the school's cafeteria.

Students at the Mary McDowell Center for Learning go on many field trips throughout the year, mainly to places that are related to the subjects they are focusing on in social studies. In addition to that, the older students go on an annual sleepover at the end of the school year to a campsite in New Jersey, where they spend two nights in cabins with their teachers and classmates and enjoy a variety of activities including swimming, rock climbing, hiking, canoeing, and archery.

The school has several annual events throughout the school year, such as Halloween festivities, a book fair, and a field day. The annual math and science fair is held on the school grounds, and children sign up for workshops taught by experts in the field as well as teachers. Families are invited to attend the Winter Fest that occurs just before the winter holidays, and the end-of-year school performance.

The school expanded its curriculum in 2005 to include a new middle school, at the same time building a brand-new greenhouse that the entire school utilizes to grow plants and conduct science experiments. The new rooftop playground has a basketball court.

The Mary McDowell Center for Learning was founded by its namesake, Mary McDowell, who was a Quaker. Her values remain today and are inherent in the school's dedication to community service, respect toward others, and peaceful conflict resolution. There is a biweekly Quaker Meeting for Worship, which takes place in the school's meeting room and is attended by the entire school. The meeting begins with a different question or statement followed by a period of silence and reflection. Subsequently, individuals may raise their hands to share their thoughts or response to the query.

Summer Program: The center offers a 2-week summer program that begins very soon after the academic school year ends in June. During this program, called Camp MarMac, students enjoy a relaxed summer atmosphere where the focus is on science and arts and crafts projects as well as field trips in Brooklyn and Manhattan.

Afterschool Programs: There is an afterschool social skills group as well as tutoring available.

Parent Involvement: There is a parent association (PA) that works on school events such as the science fair, arts and crafts fair, annual fundraising auction, and parent potluck dinners. Throughout the school year the PA sponsors family events such as baseball games, a swimming party, and arranging for guest authors to visit the classroom. Parents volunteer to run the annual holiday bazaar, gift-wrap, and pie sales. There is a bimonthly parent support group at school in the mornings.

The Mary McDowell Teaching and Learning Center (MMTLC) is an outreach program that offers various programs for parents and educators. There are professional full-day and multisession workshops for educators working with children. Past topics include understanding common learning disabilities and Orton-Gillingham workshop. The parent series is typically offered in the evening, and past topics have included strategies to help a child with homework and organizational skills, and understanding ADHD.

The school hosts an event called the Speakers Roundtable, which occurs in the fall. Parents are invited to hear experts in their field speak on subjects relevant to the school such as behavior issues, attention deficit, and learning disabilities.

School Tours: Parents should call the school to set up a tour.

Admissions Process: An interview is scheduled for your child after the school reviews your application. A current evaluation should be included. An IEP is not required.

The Application: Parents should call for a copy or complete one at the intake appointment.

Application Fee: $90

New York School for the Deaf

555 Knollwood Road
White Plains, NY 10603
Phone: (914) 949–7310
Fax: (914) 944–2331
Headmaster: John T. Tiffany, Ph.D.
Elementary Principal: Cathy Milliren
Coordinator of Clinical & Support Services: Monita Hara
E-mail: Fanwood@nysed.k12.ny.us
Web site: *www.nysd.k12.ny.us*

Grades: Nongraded

Enrollment: 58

School Year Program: 10 Month

Summer Program: No

Age Range of Students: 5–15 years

School Region: White Plains, NY

Funded for NYC: Yes

Tuition: $33,000

Financial Assistance: N/A

Classifications Accepted: Deaf and Hard of Hearing

Related Services: Occupational Therapy, Physical Therapy, Speech Therapy, and Counseling

Student–Teacher Ratios: 6:1:1, 6:1:2, and 12:1:1

Classroom Placement and Instruction: The New York School for the Deaf (NYSD; also known as Fanwood) has a program of academics, vocational training, athletics, and social activities. It is a visually oriented school, with a high priority placed on multimedia. Multisensory programs as well as smart boards programs are used to support the classroom academics. The students are encouraged to communicate through all available means, including American Sign Language (ASL) and oral English and Spanish.

The school follows the New York State curriculum, and is not graded between kindergarten through grade 6; students are grouped according to ability. The staff includes certified teachers of the deaf as well as special education teachers. There is an educational audiologist on-site, and on-site mappings by implant centers are available for children with cochlear implants.

The stated goal of NYSD is to celebrate the contributions of the deaf culture and prepare students for life in the hearing world. A number of students wear hearing aids with high-tech components. Homework is completed using keyboarding on school computers, and students can tape captioned videos in the school's TV studio. The 77-acre campus has an indoor swimming pool, sports fields, and easy access to the local community. There is a library with 12 computers, computer lab, gymnasium, and cafeteria on the premises. An art teacher visits the individual classrooms, and the school offers field trips throughout the year, beginning in the elementary grades. Various learning programs are used in the curriculum; among them are the Sundance program for reading, Mathland for mathematics, Zaner-Bloser for handwriting, Foss for science, and Harcourt Brace for social studies

Afterschool Programs: NYSD offers their students afterschool tutoring.

Parent Involvement: The school encourages parent involvement and has a parent support group.

Parent/Family Services: Sign language instruction workshops are offered to families during the school day as well as in the evenings.

School Tours: Tours of NYSD are by appointment only. Parents should bring a copy of their child's most recent audiological evaluation when they come for a tour.

The Application: Parents can contact the school to receive an application. Students must demonstrate a hearing loss of at least 80 dB HTL in the better ear in order to be considered for placement to NYSD. Besides the audiological evaluation, NYSD requires a social history, speech/language evaluation, educational evaluation, and psychological evaluation. All evaluations are available on-site. A multidisciplinary team meets to determine if NYSD is appropriate for your child. NYSD evaluates all students who apply for admission, and a child must be recommended through the CSE and have a current IEP.

Application Fee: None

The Parkside School

48 West 74th Street
New York, NY 10023
Phone: (212) 721–8888
Fax: (212) 722–1547
Administrative Director: Albina Miller
Educational Director: Leslie Thorne
Admissions: Albina Miller
E-mail: parksideschool@parksideschool.org
Web site: *www.parksideschool.org*

Grades: K–Grade 8

School Year Program: 10 Month

Age Range of Students: 5–11 years

Funded for NYC: Yes

Financial Assistance: No

Enrollment: 80

Summer Program: Yes

School Region: 10

Tuition: $31,000

Classifications Accepted: Speech Impaired (SI), Learning Disabled (LD), and Asperger's Syndrome (AS; high-functioning PDD)

Related Services: Speech Therapy, Occupational Therapy, and Counseling

Student–Teacher Ratios: 8:1:1

Classroom Placement and Instruction: Every classroom at Parkside has a visual schedule as well as a sensory toolbox. Each student has an individual performance chart on his or her desk. Classrooms have sensory tool boxes that are filled with OT items such as squeezy balls and theraputty that are used to assist children with transitions during the school day. The school is piloting a reading program, the Constable Reading Program, in which all speech therapists and teachers are trained. Handwriting Without Tears is used to teach handwriting skills in classrooms. Parkside utilizes the Stern Structural Mathematics program, which involves hands-on manipulatives for teaching math concepts and skills.

The school has a strong art program that includes fine arts and crafts. There is also a separate music program, a library with a full-time librarian, drama, and a computer room. There is a gymnasium where the children have yoga as well as gymnastic instruction with an adaptive physical education teacher.

Summer Program: Parkside has a summer program that is an extension of their school year program. Skills are reinforced during the summer and all therapies are continued. The summer program is based on themes related to New York City, with field trips twice a week.

Afterschool Programs: Afterschool activities vary each semester at Parkside. Teachers and staff initiate several programs and parents can choose a program for their child in the fall or spring.

Parent Involvement: The parent association at Parkside is very involved in fundraising as well as school events. Parents can participate in various activities, including sales of school and holiday items, the school benefit, and parent workshops. Parents also staff the school newsletter, *The Parkside Press*, which has winter and spring issues.

Parent/Family Services: Workshops for parents are available in the evening. There are parent support groups available during the school day. The Parkside Institute provides a lecture series for parents and professionals related to topics in the field of education. It also includes an outreach program for teaching professionals in the summer.

School Tours: School tours are given to parents beginning in October of each school year. Parents should call the Admissions Office to schedule attendance at one of the open houses and can also request an application at this time.

The Application: Parkside requires the following information for an application: a psychological evaluation, an educational evaluation, reports from teachers and therapists, and a current IEP. The admissions director initially screens all applications to determine if a child is appropriate for Parkside. For those children being considered, a visit to the current school setting will be made by the admissions director, beginning in January. Those children who are then being considered for placement at Parkside will be asked to visit the school for approximately 1 hour, where they will be observed. After the visit, a decision will be made within 30 days. The timeline for hearing from the Parkside is usually mid-March.

Application Fee: $75

Pathways School

291 Main Street
Eastchester, NY 10709
Phone: (914) 779–7400
Fax: (914) 779–7079
Directors: Gail Gaiser and Sue Rappaport
Web site: *www.pathwayschool.org*

Grades: K–Grade 6

Enrollment: 18

School Year Program: 10 Month

Summer Program: No

Age Range of Students: 5–12 years

School Region: Eastchester, NY

Funded for NYC: Yes

Tuition: $16,000 half-day Kindergarten (A.M./P.M.); $29,000 full-day Grades 1–6

Financial Assistance: N/A

Classifications Accepted: Pathways states that it is a school "designed specifically for students on the Autism spectrum" as well as for those "with other neurological impairments."

Related Services: Speech Therapy, Occupational Therapy, Music Therapy, Physical Therapy, and Counseling

Student–Teacher Ratios: 8:1:5

Classroom Placement and Instruction: The guiding principle of the school is to be a hands-on program for children on the Autism spectrum. The school uses TEACCH, a program developed at the University of North Carolina (www.unc.ed). Children are placed in classrooms for either half-day kindergarten (A.M. or P.M.) for 2.5 hours per day or full-day for grades 1–6. Due to the high staff-to-student ratio, academics are highly individualized. Teachers modify the New York State Learning Standards for each student. Using the TEACCH program, each child has a daily schedule, identified by icons, which can also be utilized at home. Teachers collaborate in math and language arts, and utilize a variety of programs and materials to work with the students including SRA, Edmark, and Merrill for reading, and Spectrum Math and manipulatives for math.

The students have physical education twice a week. Pathways has field trips throughout the year. In the past, students have visited the Central Park Zoo, the Planetarium, and Rye Playland.

Occupational therapy and speech are primarily "push-in," meaning that these therapies are provided within the classroom setting. Oral-motor therapy is done in individual therapy offices. Each classroom has a computer that is used to teach keyboarding skills. Other assistive technology and computer programs are also included within the daily schedule. Social skills training is determined through teacher observations and based on requests of individual parents.

Students at Pathways bring their lunch, and all classes eat together. Several classes have recess at the same time to extend social and play skills.

Afterschool Programs: There is an afterschool program from 3:00–3:30 P.M. that includes activities such as cooking and arts and crafts.

Parent Involvement: A cocktail party is held in December as a fundraising event for the school. Last year, Pathways did fundraising for new laptops and computers in every classroom.

Parent/Family Services: Each classroom is equipped with a camera, allowing parents to observe their child without interrupting the routine of the students. Home visits by staff are provided to assist with coordination of schedules and activities from home to school. Ongoing parent training is provided through workshops that present topics of relevance to Autism and parenting issues.

School Tours: Pathways has rolling admissions, so it's best to call the school to request information. Application packets will be forwarded to parents, who can then call to make an appointment to tour the school. Potential students will be interviewed at the school once the admissions application is submitted along with the application fee. A letter of acceptance or nonacceptance will be sent to parents. Students are enrolled only after being accepted and a tuition agreement has been signed by the parent and returned to Pathways with a deposit.

The Application: Parents must provide Pathways with current evaluations including psychological, speech and language, and educational testing. A social history and recent school reports are also required for applying to Pathways. When applicable, a neurological evaluation, occupational therapy, and physical therapy reports should be included as well.

Application Fee: There is a $200 nonrefundable application fee, which can be credited to future tuition.

Quality Services for the Autism Community (QSAC) Day School

12-10 150th Street
Whitestone, NY 11357
Phone: (718) 747–0136
Fax: (718) 747–6675
Day School Director: Ron Lee
Associate Executive Director: Lisa A. Veglia, CSW, MPA
Web site: *www.QSAC.com*

Grades: Nongraded

Enrollment: 33

School Year Program: 12 Month

Summer Program: Yes

Age Range of Students: 5–14 years

School Region: 75

Funded for NYC: Yes

Tuition: $30,000

Financial Assistance: N/A

Classifications Accepted: Autistic (AUT)

Related Services: Occupational Therapy, Physical Therapy, and Speech Therapy

Student–Teacher Ratios: 6:1:3

Classroom Placement and Instruction: The curriculum for reading, math, language arts, handwriting, science, and social studies at QSAC Day School is based on a variety of programs and materials such as the Edmark Program, as well as individualized programs. Teaching methods for art, music, and physical education are also individualized and are provided daily in the classroom. The school has a gymnasium, cafeteria, playground, and school store. The store is staffed by the students and teaches vocational training. The students can earn points based on daily classroom achievements and/or behavior.

All staff and therapists at QSAC Day School receive training in the principles and methods of Applied Behavior Analysis (ABA).

Summer Program: QSAC has a 6-week summer program beginning in early July. The classes are intended to be a continuation of the school year, with the same staff and same school hours.

Afterschool Programs: The QSAC Day School has an afterschool program available, where the focus is on both social and academic skills.

Parent/Family Services: Support groups for parents take place during the school day. Workshops are offered to teach parents the principles of ABA.

School Tours: Parents should call the school to schedule a tour.

The Application: Children are recommended for QSAC Day School through the CSE. Current evaluations and a current IEP must be submitted for review to determine if the program is appropriate for your child.

Application Fee: None

The Reece School

180 East 93rd Street
New York, NY 10128
(As of Sept. 2006, new address will be
25 East 104th Street, New York, NY 10029)
Phone: (212) 289–4872
Fax: (212) 423–9652
Executive Director: Dr. Thomas Colasuonno
Admissions: Jo Bellomo, Coordinator of Pupil Personnel
Services; and Barry Bullis, Educational Coordinator
E-mail: info@reeceschool.org
Web site: *www.reeceschool.org*

Grades: K–Grade 6

Enrollment: 74

School Year Program: 10 Month

Summer Program: Yes

Age Range of Students: 5–13 years

School Region: 9

Funded for NYC: Yes

Tuition: $26,000 (10 months); $3,500 (summer)

Financial Assistance: Yes

Classifications Accepted: Speech Impaired (SI), Learning Disabled (LD), Emotionally Disturbed (ED)

Related Services: Speech Therapy, Occupational Therapy, Counseling. Physical Therapy will be added in the 2006–07 school year.

Student–Teacher Ratios: 6:1:1, 8:1:1, 12:1:1 (as of 2006)

Classroom Placement and Instruction: Students have a homeroom with a 3-year age span for ages 8 and above. Within the school, teachers regroup students for language arts and math based on the functioning level of each student.

The reading curriculum includes a range of materials and programs such as Recipe for Reading, Explode the Code, and Primary Phonics. As students improve, literacy is expanded to include chapter and trade books for comprehension. In math, the Stern Structural Math and other math materials are used. Spelling is phonetically based and handwriting skills are taught using Handwriting Without Tears. Keyboarding skills are included in the curriculum beginning in kindergarten.

Social studies and science topics are sequenced and taught from kindergarten through grade 6, emphasizing vocabulary, concepts, and hands-on projects. The arts program at Reece has fine arts, clay, music, and drama/theater.

Art therapy is included to help students to express themselves using different materials successfully. Reece has a music program in which students learn to read music and play the keyboard. Adaptive physical education is available, and noncompetitive games are emphasized.

Reece has two libraries, computers in every classroom, a garden, and an art room. In 2006, they plan to have a gymnasium and cafeteria. Reece has a part-time nurse and crisis intervention staff for individual students as needed. All students participate in a positive behavior management system.

Reece will be moving into a new building in 2006, which will be barrier-free. They will continue to have the same age groupings, but will have 12 classes for a total of 90 students.

Summer Program: The Reece School has a 6-week summer school session. Along with academic instruction, students go on field trips and participate in various activities, all of which are based on a special "theme" which changes every year.

Afterschool Programs: There are no afterschool programs at this time. Reece will be adding an afterschool program in 2006.

Parent Involvement: Reece has a parent association that is involved in fundraising, school events, and other activities within the school. Parents assist with newsletters and an annual book sale. Fundraising includes sales of school items and gift items, tickets for school events, raffles, baseball games, and a friendship party. Reece is currently in a capital campaign for a new building, which will increase their total enrollment to 90 students.

Parent/Family Services: Individual counseling is available to parents as needed during the school day. Support groups focusing on social-emotional issues are provided, with a plan for these to be available in the evenings by 2006. Reece also provides a Fathers' Group. Workshops and parent training are also included in parent/family services, and generally focus on curriculum.

School Tours: Tours at Reece begin in November. At this time, parents can receive an application. Reece has three school tours each year; therefore, if you are considering Reece for your child, it is important to schedule yourself on a tour as soon as possible.

The Application: Current school reports, evaluations, and an IEP are required as part of the application packet at Reece. The admissions committee will review a child's packet only when it is complete. Students initially come to the school for an informal visit, where they will be seen by the clinical coordinator or social worker, and then work with the educational coordinator. If staff are unsure as to whether a child is appropriate for the school, they will have the child come for a half-day. Parents would be required to stay at the school during this time.

Application Fee: None

The School for Language and Communication Development (SLCD)

100 Glen Cove Avenue
Glen Cove, NY 11542
Phone: (526) 609–2000
Executive Director: Dr. Ellenmorris Tiegerman
Admissions: Dr. Helene Mermelstein
Web site: *www.slcd.org*

Grades: K–Grade 8

School Year Program: 12 Month

Age Range of Students: 5–12 years

Funded for NYC: Yes

Financial Assistance: N/A

Enrollment: 124

Summer Program: No

School Region: Glen Cove, NY

Tuition: $35,000

Classifications Accepted: Speech Impaired (SI), Learning Disabled (LD), Emotionally Disturbed (ED), Other Health Impaired (OHI), Autistic (AU), Mentally Retarded (MR), Multiple Disabilities (MD), Hearing Impaired (secondary to a language disorder)

Related Services: Speech Therapy, Occupational Therapy, Physical Therapy, Music Therapy, Dance/Movement Therapy

Student–Teacher Ratios: 6:1:1, 12:2:2

Classroom Placement and Instruction: SLCD provides a language immersion program for all of their students in order to address their language communication disorders. Students are placed in classrooms according to their language abilities and social skills.

A transdisciplinary curriculum, written by Dr. Tiegerman, allows staff to look at each child at the same time from the perspective of different disciplines (classroom/OT/speech/movement). The school has written its own curriculum, which is based on modified New York State Learning Standards. Staff use a multisensory approach as well as augmentative systems for students who require adaptive learning strategies. SLCD has an augmentative communication specialist and oral motor specialist on staff for those students who require more extensive assistance. Computers are included in every classroom, which allow occupational therapists to help students with keyboarding skills and to enhance classroom-based computer activities. Children are actively involved in communicating with their parents through an e-mail system that is part of the daily curriculum at the school.

Adaptive physical education (APE) is also available for students whose IEPs require a modified physical educational program.

Beginning in grade 4, educational subjects are departmentalized for students. This is to provide a more typical school environment for older students and to prepare them for middle school and high school. SLCD is introducing a uniform for the school, which will be phased in by 2007.

The school provides an extensive Arts program. Crafts and music (choir, piano) are provided, as well as children's clubs (recorder, photography, and publishing).

SLCD has comprehensive facilities, including a computer lab, library, gymnasium, playground, garden, art room, and cafeteria. Children bring their own lunches, but there is a full kitchen.

Afterschool Programs: Due to the time required to travel to and from SLCD, there is no afterschool program at this time. There are occasional recreational programs on weekends, run by SLCD staff.

Parent Involvement: SLCD has a Parent Teacher Friend Association (PTFA) that is actively involved in fundraising and school events. Fundraising activities that are scheduled each year include a dinner dance; raffles; and bake, plant, and candy sales. Additionally, several school events are held throughout the school year such as Casino Night, Celestial Night, and Chef Night.

Parent/Family Services: SLCD strongly believes that parents must be partners with the school. As part of their program, parents are expected to use the same materials at home as are used in their child's classroom. Parent training and counseling are also provided at the school. Individual counseling and support groups are scheduled during the school day. Workshops and training are provided four times a year, either during the school day or on a school night or weekend. These are primarily concerned with topics to help parents become more effective advocates for their children. A parent-to-parent program and buddy system has also been set up to assist parents in connecting with other parents in their district in order to provide support for parents within their individual counties.

The school psychologist counsels parents in transitioning to schools and will go to schools with parents as well as attend meetings to help parents make choices for their child's next school placement.

School Tours: Group tours are given to parents throughout the school year. Individual tours are given by a parent liaison. After the tours, parents are encouraged to look at other schools and programs in order to make an informed decision about their choice of a school for their child.

The Application: Parents can receive an application after a tour of the school. Once you have applied, an interview with the parents is scheduled first, then your child will spend a day at the school. As part of your child's interview, he/she will be evaluated by a team of school staff. This will be conducted in a classroom so that all of the professionals can observe your child at the same time in order to view your child within the same setting. A decision is made as to whether SLCD is an appropriate program for a child within 3 weeks. Parents are contacted by phone regarding acceptance. SLCD does maintain a waitlist for children.

Application Fee: $125

The Summit School

187–30 Grand Central Parkway
Jamaica Estates, NY 11432
Phone: (718) 264–2931
Fax: (718) 264–3030
Director: Judith Gordon, Ph.D.
Admissions: Judith Gordon, Ph.D.,
John Renner, Nancy Morgenroth
Web site: *www.summitschoolqueens.com*

Grades: Grades 2–12

School Year Program: 10 Month

Age Range of Students: 7–13 years

Funded for NYC: Yes

Financial Aid:

Enrollment: 120

Summer Program: No

School Region: 3

Tuition: $23,000

Classifications Accepted: Learning Disabled (LD), Emotionally Disturbed (ED)

Related Services: Occupational Therapy, Speech, and Counseling

Student–Teacher Ratios: 12:1:2

Classroom Placement and Instruction: Students are placed in classrooms based on several factors: age, gender, cognitive and language abilities, management needs, and reading and math skills. Grades 2, 4, and 8 have one classroom; grades 5 and 7 have two classrooms; grade 6 has three. The Summit School has a computer lab, library, gymnasium, art room, science lab, and swimming pool.

The goal for students at Summit is to develop strong academic skills and critical thinking skills as well as age-appropriate social skills. Summit's educational program uses multiple approaches based on students' learning styles. The reading and language arts programs are strategy-based; the math program provides hands-on instruction and manipulatives for learning. Summit also includes programs in fine art and band.

Afterschool Programs: Summit offers afterschool tutoring as well as an art and music program. Other afterschool programs are also offered depending on the age of a student, including car building, tennis, sports, drama, chorus, cooking, cartooning, weight training, and fine art programs.

Parent Involvement: Daily written communication to parents, scheduled meetings, and scheduled observations.

Parent/Family Services: Summit School has parent groups in the evenings. Workshops are provided that include guest speakers.

School Tours: Parent tours are scheduled by appointment.

The Application: Applications can be obtained by calling or by downloading the application form through the school's Web site. Parents can also complete the application at their intake appointment. Current evaluations and reports, including psychological and educational evaluations, social history, and school reports, must be submitted along with the application. The most current IEP should also be included for review.

The staff at Summit will review your child's file and determine whether your child is appropriate for the program as well as whether an appropriate class placement is available. An appointment is scheduled for children who meet these criteria to meet with the admissions team and to visit the school. Parents are contacted within a week after the interview with the decision regarding possible placement.

Application Fee: $50

West End Day School

255 West 71st Street
New York, NY 10023
Phone: (212) 873–5708
Fax: (212) 873–2345
Director: Roland Ostrower
Associate Director: Patti Wollman
Educational Head: Karalyne Sperling
Admissions: Nancy Nasr
E-mail: Info@westenddayschool.org
Web site: *www.westenddayschool.org*

Grades: K–Grade 6

Enrollment: 55

School Year Program: 10 Month

Summer Program: Yes

Age Range of Students: 5–12 years

School Region: 10

Funded for NYC: No

Tuition: $28,500 (10 months); $2,500 (summer program)

Financial Assistance: No

Classifications Accepted: Speech Impaired (SI), Learning Disabled (LD), Emotionally Disturbed (ED) or emotionally/socially vulnerable, Other Health Impaired (OHI)

Related Services: Speech Therapy, Occupational Therapy, Counseling

Student–Teacher Ratios: 10:1:1

Classroom Placement and Instruction: Children are combined by ages across 2 years in classrooms, beginning with a 5–6-year-old class and ending with an 11–12-year-old class, from kindergarten through grade 6. West End Day uses the New York State Learning Standards as a guideline for their curriculum as well as other curriculum and materials. In reading, Scholastic Literacy Place and Orton-Gillingham-based programs are used with students. Stern Mathematics is utilized for math applications. For handwriting, West End Day uses Handwriting Without Tears and Orton-Gillingham. Language arts, social studies, science, and PE/APE focus on the New York State Learning Standards for curriculum goals. The arts program includes fine arts, music, and drama/theater. Yoga and chess are also incorporated within the school day for students. West End Day has a computer room, library, art room, gymnasium, and outdoor space for students.

Social skills are taught as part of the curriculum at West End Day, and students receive play therapy/counseling as part of their daily program.

Summer Program: West End Day has a Summer Learning Program that integrates activities in language arts, movement, art, cooking, field trips, and swimming. It is a 6-week program provided in small structured groups, beginning in July. The cost is $2,500.

Afterschool Programs: West End Day has an afterschool program, which is supervised by several staff members. Rollerblading, swimming, yoga, computer, cooking, drama, and homework/study skills are some of the activities provided.

Parent Involvement: There is a parent association that handles fundraising activities for the school. These include sales of school items and gift items, a school benefit, and a spring family cruise. The parent association at West End Day also works on school events throughout the school year.

Parent/Family Services: Individual counseling and support groups are available to parents. Both are provided during the school day, and parents can also receive counseling in the evenings. Individual parent and parent/child sessions aimed at clarifying stresses and how to handle them are part of parent/family services. Workshops and parent training are presented in the evenings at West End Day. A variety of parent workshops/training have been provided related to how to "see" and talk to your child.

School Tours: Parents should call the admissions director to schedule a tour of West End Day and to receive an application. Tours begin in October and are provided throughout the school year.

The Application: West End Day requires a neuropsychological or psychoeducational evaluation, an educational report, and immunization records for application to the school. If your child receives therapy, reports from each area should also be included in your packet. For younger children (5–7 years) who are being considered for placement, a staff member will observe them at their current school if the school is located in Manhattan. Older students being considered for placement are invited to visit West End Day for a full day. Parents will be contacted at the end of the observation or visit regarding their child's placement at West End Day.

Application Fee: $50

Windward School

40 West Red Oak Lane
White Plains, NY 10604–3602
Phone: (914) 949–6968
Fax: (914) 949–8220
Head: Dr. James E. Van Amburg
Admissions: Maureen A. Sweeney
Web site: *www.windward-school.org*

Grades: Grades 1–9

School Year Program: 10 Month

Age Range of Students: 6–14 years

Funded for NYC: No

Financial Assistance: Yes

Enrollment: 368

Summer Program: Yes

School Region: White Plains, NY

Tuition: $34,750

Classifications Accepted: Learning Disabled (LD) or written diagnosis of language disability

Related Services: Individualized therapy is not provided. Speech therapists and a psychologist work with groups and help with the classroom programs.

Student–Teacher Ratios: 12:1:1

Classroom Placement and Instruction: Windward emphasizes the remediation of learning/language disabilities and has developed a core curriculum designed to meet the needs of its students. Teachers use a language-based curriculum that emphasizes listening, speaking, reading, and writing. Students are taught to read, write, and spell through Orton-Gillingham methods. Instruction is individualized and highly structured in order for students to progress at their own rate of learning.

Organizational and study skills, developing problem-solving strategies, and general knowledge are also emphasized at Windward. Windward maintains high academic standards and follows the New York State Learning Standards.

Summer Program: The summer program at Windward provides three weeks of instruction (morning) or enrichment (afternoon). The mornings are devoted to math, science, or study skills. In the afternoons, students can choose either sports or art activities.

Afterschool Programs: Windward has an afterschool program that offers athletics as well as enrichment activities (art, computer) for the lower school students (grades 1 through 4). Interscholastic sports are available for middle school students.

Parent Involvement: Windward has an active parents association. The PTA welcomes new families by having current parents act as mentors to new parents. Additionally, parents can participate in the Teacher Institute at Windward, attend guest lectures during the day and in the evenings, and work as volunteers for fundraising events such as the annual benefit/auction.

Parent/Family Services: Individual parent–teacher conferences, workshops on topics related to learning disabilities, and an outreach program are provided through Windward to help parents better understand their child.

Windward's outreach program is available to the community as well as to professionals. The school has a Teacher Training Institute that provides lectures, courses, and workshops to educators and professionals.

School Tours: Before calling for an appointment, you should determine if your child meets the criteria for admission to Windward. Windward requires that a child have a written diagnosis of a language/or learning disability that includes at least average to superior intellectual potential. Additionally, Windward does not accept any children with behavioral or emotional difficulties that would interfere with classroom instruction.

The admissions process usually involves attendance at an information session at the school. Parents should call the admission office for an appointment and request an application at this time if they feel that their child might be appropriate.

The Application: Windward requires a psychoeducational evaluation (within 2 years) as well as projective testing for students to be considered. Recent school reports, a release form, and a completed application must be sent to complete your child's file. The admission committee will review an a child's file only after all of the information is forwarded.

If your child is invited to interview at Windward, there is an additional $200 fee to screen your child. The screening involves the child spending time in a classroom as well with a learning specialist. Within 2 weeks of the screening, the admission committee will present their findings and recommendations to you. If your child is recommended for acceptance, you will receive a contract at a later date. If your child is not accepted, the committee will suggest other options to you.

Application Fee: $50

Winston Preparatory School

126 West 17th Street
New York, NY 10011
Phone: (646) 638–2705
Fax: (646) 638–2706
Headmaster: Dr. Scott Bezsylko
Admissions Director: Erinn Skeffington
E-mail: admissions@winstonprep.edu
Web site: *www.winstonprep.edu*

Grades: Grades 6–12

School Year Program: 10 Month

Age Range of Students: 11–19 years

Funded for NYC: No

Enrollment: 220

Summer Program: Yes

School Region: 10

Tuition: $36,750

Financial Assistance: Yes. Families must submit a School and Student Service (SSS) form to be considered for financial aid. The school will use this information as a guideline for financial aid to a family.

Classifications Accepted: Learning Disabled (LD), Speech Impaired (SI)

Related Services: Speech Therapy

Student–Teacher Ratios: 12:1 for classes; the Focus Program provides a 1:1 daily session for 40 minutes with a specialist as part of each student's daily schedule.

Classroom Placement and Instruction: Classes are mixed-age groups based on individual learning profiles, not grade levels. Children may be placed according to the following age groups: 11–13 years, 12–14 years, and 12–15 years. Winston Prep uses the following curriculum and programs for instruction: Preventing Academic Failure (Orton-Gillingham) and Wilson Reading Program and Diana Hanbury King (handwriting). The school has a gymnasium and an art room. The art program includes ceramics and crafts as well as drama/theater.

Summer Program: Winston offers a summer program for an additional fee, for 1 month in June, which focuses on academics and follows the curriculum of the school year.

Afterschool Programs: The Learning Support Center Program provides afterschool services in academics, speech/language therapy, and other educational support for grade 6–12 students. There are two options for students, an individual option and a group option. Individual sessions focus on targeted areas of learning that a student needs to strengthen. The program also has language-based pragmatic groups to "practice and enhance their interpersonal skills." Students are taught by professionals such as learning specialists, speech therapists, reading specialists, and content instructors to work with students.

Parent Involvement: The parent association at Winston Prep assists the school in fundraising, school events, parent workshops, and student-directed events and parties. Fundraising activities include sale of school items and gift items, a school benefit, and an annual gala. Winston Prep also sends an annual appeal letter to parents, friends, and alumni.

Parent/Family Services: Individual counseling is available for parents as well as workshops and training. Winston Prep has provided workshops in social/emotional issues related to LD children as well as workshops related to learning disabilities and language, nonverbal learning disabilities, and executive functioning disorders.

School Tours: Parents must register via e-mail with the assistant director of admissions to attend an open house at Winston Prep. Parents are required to attend an open house in order for their child to be considered for admission. During an open house, parents will be able to tour Winston Prep, observe students and classes, and ask questions regarding the admission process to the school.

The Application: The admissions committee will review your child's application only after they have received all materials required. Within 2 weeks from the initial screening of the committee, you will be notified as to whether they think your child is appropriate for Winston Prep. At that time, your child will be invited for a school visit. During your child's visit, there will be further testing conducted, and your child will spend time in a classroom and will be interviewed by the school deans. Winston Prep will notify parents of any child who is not considered appropriate for the school by mail.

The following information is required for an application to be considered complete at Winston Prep: a psychological evaluation including personality functioning (Rorschach and/or the Thematic Apperception Test), parent questionnaire, teacher or specialist recommendation, and school transcripts (current school reports) with release form.

Application Fee: $70

Yeshiva Education for Special Students (YESS!)

147-37 70th Road
Kew Gardens Hills, NY 11367
Phone: (718) 268–5976
Fax: (718) 268–2933
Director: Rabbi Yaakov Lustig
Admissions Director: Rabbi Yaakov Lustig
E-mail: yess@acninc.net
Web site: *www.bjeny.org*

Grades: Nongraded

School Year Program: 10 Month

Age Range of Students: 5–14 years

Tuition: $23,500

Enrollment: 23

Summer Program: No

School Region: 3

Funded for NYC: No

Financial Assistance: Financial assistance is available on an individual/ family income basis.

Classifications Accepted: Learning Disabled (LD), Speech Impaired (SI), Other Health Impaired (OHI)

Related Services: Speech Therapy, Occupational Therapy, Physical Therapy, and Counseling

Student–Teacher Ratios: Classes have no more than eight children with a student-to-teacher ratio of 3:1 or 4:1.

Classroom Placement and Instruction: YESS! offers a full curriculum in both general and Judaic studies. Classes are grouped in a combined grade structure, within three grade levels. Placement is determined by the director and teachers based on a child's academic and social needs. The classroom instruction is highly individualized in order to best support each student's learning ability. The school has a balanced approach to teaching reading, including whole language and elements of Orton-Gillingham and Wilson programs. Other programs used include Handwriting Without Tears for handwriting, and Steck Vaughn materials for science and social studies. All classes are language-based and multisensory to encourage cognitive and social emotional development. Some of the students at YESS! attend art, music and physical education classes in the yeshiva of central Queens.

The school has a small library, and has use of the Yeshiva School library as well. There is a computer room, playground, and cafeteria at the school.

YESS! is located on the third floor of the Yeshiva School. School begins at 8:00 A.M. daily with Tefillah, and classes are dismissed at 1:30 P.M. on Fridays.

Afterschool Programs: There are no afterschool programs at YESS!

Parent Involvement. There is a parent association involved in fundraising and school events. Each year there is a school benefit, which is the school's biggest fundraiser. Raffles, the sale of school items, and an annual appeal letter are all part of fundraising at the school.

Parent/Family Services: There are evening workshops offered that focus primarily on parenting issues.

School Tours: Tours are available by appointment. Parents should call the school to schedule a meeting with the director.

The Application: After meeting with the director, you will be given an application and a release form. Current psychological, educational, speech, and occupational therapy evaluations should be returned with your application. The director and consulting special educational professionals will review each child's packet. If your child is appropriate for admission to YESS! he/she will have a brief intake screening at the school. You will be notified shortly after if your child is accepted to the school.

Application Fee: $100

PART IV

Resources

There are many medical professionals, therapists, educators, and resource centers in New York City for families with children with special needs. In the course of writing this book we decided to ask the families who actually use these services and whose children work with these professionals for their recommendations.

We've listed those individuals and agencies that were recommended by parents who completed our parent survey. This listing is our version of the playground grapevine that parents have, relied on for so many years. Obviously, what works beautifully for one child may not even remotely work for another. Over and over again we encountered parents who went out of their way to share a personal experience and recommend a professional they had consulted for their child with special needs. With this information we have created a unique list, every single recommendation coming from a parent who personally had a positive and in many cases ongoing experience under their medical care or educational expertise.

We have, created six different listings in this resources section: Therapists, Evaluation Centers, Medical Professionals, Afterschool and Summer Camp, Recommended Web Sites, and Attorneys. We hope that this will be helpful to those of you who continue to search for the support you need.

EVALUATION CENTERS

Center-Based

Bank Street Family Center
610 West 112th St., NYC 10025
(212) 875-4412

Child Development Center
*Jewish Board of Family & Children's
Services, Marian Davidson-Amadeo,
CSW, Director*
120 West 57th St., NYC 10019
(212) 632-4733

**HASC (Hebrew Academy for Special
Children)**
5902 14th Ave., Brooklyn, NY 11219

The League for the Hard of Hearing
50 Broadway, 6th fl., NYC 10004
(917) 305-7766

**Lenox Hill Hospital Center for
Attention & Learning Disorders**
1430 Second Ave., NYC 10021
(212) 434-4594

**Marathon Infants & Toddlers
Programs**
220-18 Horace Harding Expwy,
Bayside, NY 11364
(718) 423-0056

NYU Child Study Center
577 First Ave., NYC 10016
(212) 263-6622

**Elizabeth W. Pouch Center for
Special People**
657 Castleton Ave., Staten Island,
NY 10301
(718) 448-9775

**Rusk Institute of Rehabilitation
Medicine**
400 East 34th St., NYC 10016
(212) 263-6034/6037

These Our Treasures (TOT)
2778 Bruckner Blvd., Bronx, NY 10465

Private

Marilyn Agin, M.D.
Developmental Pediatrician
79 Laight St., #1A, NYC 10013
(212) 274-9180

Steven Alter, Ph.D.
117 West 72nd St., Ste. 5E, NYC 10023
(646) 872-6229
110-45 Queens Blvd., Ste. A2, Forest
Hills, NY 11375
(718) 261-3363

Elizabeth Auricchio
5 East 78th St., NYC 10021
(212) 228-9350

Dr. Helen Auricchio
Educational Evaluator
5 East 78th St., NYC 10021
(212) 228-9350/879-9046

Dr. Gail Bedi
Pediatric Neurology
171 East 74th St., Ste. C2, NYC 10021
(212) 288-1001

Dr. Vickie Beech, Ph.D.
3 East 68th St., NYC 10021
(212) 628-9200 ext.103

Steven Blaustein, Ph.D.
Speech Pathologist
17 East 97th St., NYC 10029
(212) 876-0357

Janet Brain
Educational Evaluator
2 East 84th St., NYC 10028
(212) 650-0016

Dr. Alizah Brozgold
*St. Vincent's Hospital, Dept of
Rehabilitation Medicine*
170 West 12th St., NYC 10011
(212) 604-7155

Child Development Center
South Miami Hospital
6200 SW 73rd St., South Miami, FL
33143
(786) 662-4000

**Children's Evaluation and
Rehabilitation Center**
Albert Einstein College of Medicine
1410 Pelham Pkwy South, Bronx, NY
10461
(718) 430–8500

William Dince, Ph.D.
5 East 76th St., NYC 10021
(212) 535–7350

Lisa Dubinsky, Psy.D.
48 West 21st St., NYC 10010
(646) 336–6804

Dr. Nancy Eng
185 Canal St., 6th fl., NYC 10013
(212) 343–7323

Arlene Falk
1025 Fifth Ave., NYC 10028
(212) 734–1117

Dr. Ellen Farber
200 East 94th St., Ste. 1611, NYC
10128
(212) 987–5651

Dr. Mark Freilich
Total Kids Developmental Pediatrics
205 West End Ave., NYC 10023
(212) 787–2148

Dr. Muriel Frischer
54 Montgomery Pl., Brooklyn, NY
11215
(718) 857–8310

Dr. Gail Goldman, Ph.D.
180 East 79th St., NYC 10021
(212) 744–3700

Shoshana Goldman, Ph.D.
451 West End Ave., NYC 10024
(212) 362–3071

Dr. Karen Hopkins
*NYU Medical Center Developmental
Behavioral Pediatrics*
503 First Ave., Ste. 3A, NYC 10016
(212) 562–4313

Dr. David Kaufman
Neurology
3 East 83rd St., NYC 10028
(212) 737–4911

Ruth Landstrom, Ph.D.
344 West 72nd St., NYC 10023
(212) 721–0499

Fern Leventhal
New York University
550 First Ave., Rm. 212, NYC
10016
(212) 263–7753

Antoinette Lynn, Ph.D.
277 West End Ave., NYC 10023
(212) 724–7246

**Manhattan Eye, Ear, and Throat
Hospital**
210 East 64 St., NYC 10021
(212) 605–3788
Children's Hearing Institute
(212) 605–3794
Cochlear Implant Center
(212) 605–3793
Communication Disorders
(212) 605–3740

Dr. Cecilia McCarton
The McCarton Center
350 East 82nd St., NYC 10028
(212) 996–9019

Andrew Morrel, Ph.D.
140 West 79th St., NYC 10024
(212) 721–3710

Judith Moskowitz,
*Psychoeducational Evaluations,
Mt. Sinai*
547 Saw Mill River Rd., Ardsley, NY
10502
(914) 674–0354

NYU Child Study Center
Tisch Hospital
550 First Ave., NYC 10016
(212) 263–6622

Donna Orloff
Speech Pathologist
45 East 74th St., NYC 10021
(212) 794–3269

Dr. Sonia Orenstein
241 Central Park West, #1D, NYC
10024
(212) 595–4041

Janine Pollack
LAMM Institute
110 Amity St., Brooklyn, NY 11201
(718) 638–0168

Dr. Valerie Raymond
510 East 86th St., NYC 10028
(212) 439–9567

June Russo
121 Madison Ave., NYC 10016
(212) 679–0511

Dr. David Salsberg
Rusk Institute
60 Madison Ave., #907, NYC
10010
(212) 263–6168

Susan T. Schwartz, Ph.D.
1160 5th Ave., Ste. 109, NYC 10029
(212) 426–0232

Dr. Michele Shackelford, Ph.D.
*Lenox Hill Hospital Center for Attention
& Learning Disorders (CALD)*
1430 Second Ave., NYC 10021
(212) 434–4594

Dr. Elizabeth Sharpless
*Psychoeducational evaluations; Career
counseling; Counseling for children,
teens, & families*
24 East 12th St., Ste. 502, NYC
10003
(212) 727–8131

Dr. Margaret Snow
55 East 72nd St., #8S, NYC 10021
(212) 861–4800

Soifer Center
333 Old Tarrytown Rd., White Plains,
NY 10603
(914) 683–5401

William Solodow
127 West 79th St., #3, NYC, 10024
(212) 787–4681

**SPOTS (Special Programs in
Occupational Therapy Services)**
611 Broadway, Ste. 902, NYC 10012
(212) 473–0011

Dr. Anne Steinberg
999 Fifth Ave., NYC 10028
(212) 472–7536

Barbara Wolf-Dorlester, Ph.D.
145 West 96th St., NYC, 10025
(212) 749–4457

Dr. Donna Zanolla
2600 Netherlands Ave., Ste. 108,
Riverdale, NY 10463
(212) 642–5849

Agencies

**The Cooke Center for Learning &
Development**
475 Riverside Dr., Ste. 703, NYC
10115
(212) 280–4473

Easter Seals NYC
11 West 42nd St., 30th fl., NYC
10036
(212) 398–0648

**Jewish Board of Family & Children's
Services**
120 West 57th St., NYC 10019
(212) 582–9100; (888) 523–2769

Theracare
116 West 32nd St., 8th fl., NYC
10001
(212) 564–2350

TIPSE (Toddler Infant Program for Special Education)
329 Norway Ave., Staten Island, NY 10305
(718) 987–9400

YAI/National Institute for People with Disabilites Network
460 West 34th St., NYC 10001
(212) 273–6100

Hospitals and Clinics

Beth Israel Medical Center
Speech Language Department, Phillips Ambulatory Care Center
10 Union Sq, Ste. 2K, NYC 10003
(212) 844–8430

Blythedale Children's Hospital
Bradhurst Ave., Valhalla, NY 10595
(914) 592–7555

Dr. Kwame Anyane-Yeboa
Columbia Presbyterian Genetics Dept
3959 Broadway, 6 North, Rm. 601A, NYC 10032
(212) 305–6731

Dr. Orrin Devinsky
Comprehensive Epilepsy Center, NYU Medical Center
403 East 34th St., 4th fl., NYC 10016
(212) 263–8871

Hunterdon Medical Center Child Evaluation & Treatment
2100 Wescott Dr., Flemington, NJ 08822
(908) 788–6396

Kennedy Child Study Center
151 East 67th St., NYC 10021
(212) 988–9500

LAMM Institute
110 Amity St., Brooklyn, NY 11201
(718) 638–0168

Lenox Hill Hospital
110 East 77th St., NYC 10021
(212) 434–2000

Long Island University
720 Northern Blvd., Brookville, NY 11548
(516) 299–2000

Children's Hospital at Montefiore
3415 Bainbridge Ave., Bronx, NY 10467
(718) 741–2426

Children's Hospital of New York-Presbyterian
3959 Broadway, NYC 10032
(212) 305–5437

New York Weill Cornell Children's Hospital
525 East 68th St., NYC 10021
(212) 746–5454

NYU Medical Center
550 First Ave., NYC 10016
(212) 263–7300

Dr. Janine Pollack
710 West End Ave., NYC 10025
(212) 222–6070

Dr. David Salsberg
Rusk Institute
60 Madison Ave., #907, NYC 10010
(212) 263–6168

Ryan Community Health Center
110 West 97th St., NYC 10025
(212) 749–1820

St. Vincent's Hospital
170 West 12th St., NYC 10011
(212) 604–7000

Schneider Children's Hospital
Long Island Jewish Hospital
69–01 76th Ave., New Hyde Park, NY 11040
(516) 470–3000

Dr. Agnes Whitaker
Director, Developmental Neuropsychiatry
Program for Autism and Related
Disorders at New York-Presbyterian
Columbia University Medical Center
635 West 165th St., Rm. 635, NYC
10032
(212) 342–1600

Other

Louise Levy at Beth Israel Hospital
210 East 64th St., NYC 10021
(212) 605–3793
863 Park Ave., Ste. 1E, NYC 10021
(212) 319–8423

Special Sprouts Nursery School
446 6th Ave., Brooklyn, NY 11215
(718) 965–8573

SUNY Optometrics
33 West 42nd St., NYC 10036
(212) 780–4950

Westchester Institute for Human Development
Child Development Services
Cedarwood Hall, Valhalla, NY 10595
(914) 493–5246

THERAPISTS

Occupational Therapists

Adler, Molly, Gurland, & Associates LLC
412 Ave. of the Americas, NYC 10011
(212) 477–4878; (212) 477–9838

Steven Alter, Ph.D.
117 West 72nd St., Ste. 5E, NYC
10023
(646) 872–6229
110–45 Queens Blvd., Ste. A2, Forest
Hills, NY 11375
(718) 261–3363

Joan Avalone
39 West 14th St., Ste. 307, NYC
10011

Arlene Baily
740 West End Ave., Ste. 2, NYC
10025
(212) 663–3331; (212) 663–3380

Marjorie Becker-Lewin, OTR
144 West 86th St., Ste. 1B, NYC
10024
(212) 595–7789

Michelle Biro Deitch, MS, OTR/L
740 West End Ave., #3, NYC 10025
(212) 665–5119

Lisa Burton
Sage Center for Children
140 West End Ave., 1G, 10023
(212) 787–4086

Sandra Reis Cooper
Sage Center for Children
140 West End Ave., NYC 10023
(212) 787–4086

Sharon Davis, OTR, Handwriting
145 West 96th St., NYC 10025
(212) 749–4303

Kirsten DeBear, OTR
545 West End Ave., NYC 10024
(212) 877–8242

Larry Deemer
SPOTS (Special Programs in
Occupational Therapy Services)
611 Broadway, Ste. 902, NYC 10012
(212) 473–0011

Tina Efron, OT/L
Fine Motor & Handwriting
407 6th Ave., #1, Brooklyn, NY
11215
(718) 369–6998; (718) 651–3788

Stacy Eisenberg
500 East 83rd St., #4L, NYC 10028
(917) 509–6570

Ann Feldman, OTR/L
Occupational Therapy & MA Dance Instruction
Various locations
(917) 355–7115
(718) 796–6540

Fine & Gross Motor Skills
2 Hickory Rd., Westport, CT 06880
(203) 434–9134

Anna Friedman, Stephen Gaynor
Total Kids Developmental Pediatrics
205 West End Ave., NYC 10023
(212) 787–2148

Vanessa Giardena
250 5th Ave., Ste. 201, NYC 10001
(212) 685–3266

Maha Anand Golden
496 Hudson St., NYC 10014
(212) 627–4321

Prudence Heisler
SPOTS (Special Programs in Occupational Therapy Services)
611 Broadway, Ste. 902, NYC 10012
(212) 473–0011

Robyn Heller
Rusk Institute
400 East 34th St., 5th fl., NYC 10016
(212) 263–6013

Elise Henry, OTR/L
Kids in Motion OT, PLLC
2735 Henry Hudson Pkwy West, Bronx, NY 10463
(718) 601–7400

Iné Hubers
The LAB
97th and West End Ave., NYC 10024
(646) 283–4546

Marie Leo, MA, OTR
Sensory Integration
111 West 94th St., #FB, NYC 10025
(212) 866–9566

Jennifer Levin
535 East 70th St., NYC 10021
(212) 606–1368

Tori Lingen
Children's Speech and Rehabilitation Therapist
7 Noel Lane, Jericho, NY 11753
(516) 827–1970

Susan Lubrano
Therapy Services of Greater NY
45 North Station Plaza, Ste 203, Great Neck, NY 11021
(516) 482–2650

Elizabeth (Betsy) Lychak
246 West 80th St., NYC 10024
(212) 362–3530

Elizabeth Maglari
Manhattan East Associates
1675 York Ave., NYC 10128
(212) 410–4000

Paula McCreedy
SPOTS (Special Programs in Occupational Therapy Services)
611 Broadway, Ste. 902, NYC 10012
(212) 473–0011

Kathleen McGovern
(also does craniosacral therapy)
(212) 670–0529

Metropolitan Center Mental Health
160 West 86th St., NYC 10024
(212) 362–8755

Margaret Palazzolo
Special Steps
519 Broadway, Staten Island, NY 10310
(718) 948–8879

Sheri Perlman
41 West 72nd St., NYC 10023
(212) 721–6877

Jayme Lewin Rich,MTA, OTR/L
Integrative Pediatrics
39 West 14th St., Ste. 307, NYC
10011
(212) 414–2777

Lori Rothman, OTR
144 West 86th St., #1B, NYC 10024
(212) 595–7782

Linda Rowe
Support by Design
143 Reade St., NYC 10013
(212) 964–9252
69 Murray St., NYC 10007
(212) 608–9660

Loren Shlaes
39 West 14th St., Ste. 307, NYC 10011
(347) 276–0632

Dr. Jordana Skurka
51 East 12th St., 5th fl., NYC 10003
(212) 645–5810

Sheri Stein-Bellow/Jude Deprosa
284 Watchogue Rd., Staten Island,
10314
(718) 698–6866

Elyse Stern, Pediatric OT
Manhattan East Associates
1675 York Ave., Ste. P-1A, NYC
10128
(212) 410–3089

Rhoda Stern
201 East 17th St., NYC 10003
(212) 673–0848

Carrie Stranch, OT
*Sensory Processing, Preemies, Infants,
Private Home-based Therapy*
(212) 647–0427; (917) 273–2256

Support by Design
143 Reade St., NYC 10013
(212) 964–9252
69 Murray St., NYC 10007
(212) 608–9660

Margaret Tumelty, MS, OTR, BCP
*Sensory Processing Disorders, Home-
based Therapy*
(516) 242–0001

Susan Wagler
69-38 180th St., Flushing, NY
11365
(718) 591–3976

Jen Jacobs Wein, OTR/L
Home-based Therapy
(917) 846–4576

**Westchester Occupational Therapy
Associates**
200 Business Park Dr., Ste. 301,
Armonk, NY 10504
(914) 730–0210

Dr. Margaret Wolder, Ph.D.
200 West 86th St., Ste. 1J, NYC
10024
(212) 724–8362

**Jessica Semeyram Wortman, MA
OTR/L**
*Sensory Integration, Therapeutic
Listening*
70 West 83rd St., #DA, NYC 10024
(917) 881–3585

Speech/Language Pathologists

Suzanne Abrams
50 West 72nd St., Apt. #11D, NYC
10023
(212) 799–6677

Dr. Marilyn Agin
79 Laight St., #1A, NYC 10013
(212) 274–9180

Melissa Young Alford
All About Kids
255 Executive Dr., #LI102, Plainview,
NY 11803
(516) 576–2040

Amy Belkin
Total Kids Developmental Pediatrics
205 West End Ave., NYC 10023
(212) 544–7441

Steven Blaustein, Ph.D.
Speech Pathologist
17 East 97th St., NYC 10029
(212) 876–0357

Michele Bogaty-Blend
Cochlear Implant Center, New York Eye and Ear Infirmary
310 East 14th St., NYC 10003
(212) 605–3793

Beth Brenzel
935 Park Avenue, Ste. 1D, NYC 10028
(212) 585–1886

Lisa Brideson-Glynn
Oral-motor & Feeding Specialist
133 East 73rd St., NYC, 10021
(212) 734–4112; (212) 249–6743

Michelle De Maria
Children's Speech and Rehabilitation Therapists
7 Noel Lane, Jericho, NY 11753
(516) 827–1970

Nancy Dryfuss
425 East 63rd St., NYC 10021
(212) 593–4665

Mrs. Dunetz, Mrs. Laskin
School for Language & Communication Development
100 Glen Cove Ave., Glen Cove, NY 11542
(516) 609–2000

Stacy Eisenberg
500 East 83rd St., #4L, NYC 10028
(917) 509–6570

Phyllis Fabricant
80 East End Ave., NYC 10028
(212) 628–4708

Arlene Falk
1025 Fifth Ave., NYC 10028
(212) 734–1117

Rachel Fisch-Kaplan
107 West 82nd St., Ste. 103, NYC 10024
(212) 712–2014

LeAnne Franzreb
Rusk Institute
400 East 34th St., NYC 10016
(212) 263–6026

Ann Frelich, SLP
88 Bleecker St., #1D, NYC 10012
(212) 475–7331

Stacey Garsson
Preschool and School-Age Language Development, Language Groups, Articulation, & Fast ForWord
425 East 86th St., Ste. 1A, NYC 10028
(212) 427–7667

Dr. Donna Geffner
St. Johns University Speech & Hearing Center
8000 Utopia Pkwy., Queens, NY 11439
(718) 990–6480

Elaine Glazer
29 Glen Cove Dr, Glen Head, NY 11545
(516) 671–1224

Judith Gold
903 Park Ave., NYC 10021
(212) 472–7734

Deborah Gottlieb
114 East 71st St., NYC 10021
(212) 737–7469

Debra Hagen
Pediatric Associates for Language and Speech
333 West 57th St., NYC 10019
(212) 245–2455

Bethe Halligan
67 St. Marks Pl., NYC 10003
(212) 473–4714

Colleen Houston
34 Wildwood Rd., Chappaqua, NY
10514
(914) 238–3747

Randy Jacoby, MS, CCC, SLP
*Pediatrics, PDD, Articulation, Language-
based Learning Disabilities, Neuromotor &
Oral-motor Issues, Hearing Impairments*
182 East 79th St., Ste. C, NYC
10021
(212) 772–2238

Jennifer Kaplan
Rusk Institute
(212) 263–6026

Patricia Walsh Kay
935 Park Ave., NYC 10028
(212) 472–1910

Risa Kirsh/Rachel Wodin
114 East 71st St., NYC 10021
(212) 327–1400

Carol Lampert-Barrish, Ph.D.
305 East 86th St., NYC 10028
(212) 427–6032

Sharyn Lico
401 East 81st St., NYC 10028
(212) 861–5871, (212) 628–3560

Tori Lingen
*Children's Speech and Rehabilitation
Therapists*
7 Noel Lane, Jericho, NY 11753
(516) 827–1970

Susana Wan Linker
99 Battery Place, #5-D, NYC
10280
(917) 488–8835

Karen Louick, Speech Pathology
17 7th Ave., Brooklyn, NY 11217
(718) 638–0168

**Manhattan Eye, Ear, and Throat
Hospital**
Speech Clinic
210 East 64th St., NYC 10021
(212) 605–3796

Susan Mason
412 Sixth Ave., Ste. 710, NYC
10011
(212) 691–1806

Gail Merrefield
284 Watchogue Rd., Staten Island,
NY 10314
(718) 698–6866

**Edward D. Mysak Speech and
Language Clinic**
Teachers College, Columbia University
525 West 120th St., Macy Hall,
Room 169, NYC 10027
(212) 678–3409

**North Shore Speech and Language
Associates**
444 Community Dr # 309,
Manhasset, NY 11030
(516) 627–5546

Donna Orloff
45 East 74th St., NYC 10021
(212) 794–3269

Patricia Peifer
50 Walker Street #3-A, NYC 10013
(212) 625–8252; (917) 743–1150

John Pistasio
(917) 697–9178

Margery Rappaport
(212) 369–9300

Marissa Ramos
(718) 948–8879

Fran Redstone
(917) 750–0052

Michelle Rubinov
(212) 794–3269

Beatrice Schreter
311 East 72nd St., NYC 10021
(212) 249–5636

Dr. Cecile Stein
(914) 761–2396

Melinda Velez
(917) 379–9759

Heidi Volosov
(212) 245–7369

Erica Wasserman
82 Apple Ln., Briarcliff Manor, NY
10510
(917) 806–5292

Allison Weinstein
1 Tiffany Pl., Brooklyn, NY 11231
(718) 858–6060

Dr. Pia Wikstrom
Manhattan Speech & Language
50 West 72nd St., NYC 10023
(212) 724–2580

Dr. Elaine Yukelvich
48 West 21st St., Ste. 301, NYC
10010
(212) 989–3689

Physical Therapists

Lisa Haid
Private Contractor
(203) 869–8350

Cheryl Hall
*Children's Speech and Rehabilitation
Therapy*
7 Noel Ln., Jericho, NY 11753
(516) 827–1970

Counseling/Play Therapists

Ron Balamuth
393 West End Ave., NYC 10024
(212) 877–1118

Sheri Baron
185 Millwood Rd., Chappaqua, NY
10514
(914) 762–2058

Ronnie Beecher
200 Park Ave. South, Ste. 916, NYC
10003
(212) 505–1441

Dr. Bette Clark
127 West 79th St., NYC 10024
(212) 362–6759

Susan Cohen
500 West End Ave., NYC 10024
(212) 595–9549

Darcy Dean
230 West 13th St., NYC 10011
(212) 741–5182; (212) 741–5182

Dr. Norma Doft
295 Central Park West, #4A, NYC
10024 (212) 787–5046

Dr. Nancy Eppler Wolff
107 West 86th St., NYC 10024
(212) 595–5070

Dr. Anne Erreich
170 West End Ave., NYC 10023
(212) 496–2155

Diana Feit, Ph.D.
201 East 87th St., NYC 10128
(212) 722–2639

Ana Lisa Fredrickson
133 East 72nd St., Ste. 412, NYC
10021
(347) 661–7660

Lisa Frenette-Flemma
Behavioral Therapy
133 East 73rd St., NYC 10021
(212) 988–4800

Steven Friedfeld
231 East 76th St., Ste. 1K, NYC 10021
(212) 744–8737

Dr. Richard Gallagher
NYU Child Study Center
577 First Ave., NYC 10016
(212) 263–6622

Todd Germain
Practice for Reflective Parenting
27 West 72nd St., Ste. 707, NYC
10023
(212) 496–2889

Ronnie Goldblatt
The Churchill School & Center
301 East 29th St., NYC 10016
(212) 722–0610

Dr. Deansin Goodson-Parker
30 East 76th St., 4th fl., NYC 10021
(212) 717–5273; (212) 988–0898

Sandy Greenbaum
Peer Playgroup
182 East 79th St., Ste. A, NYC 10021
(212) 717–4452; toll free (877)
787–2343

Dr. Sky Haverman
140 West End Ave., #1G, NYC 10023
(212) 875–4572

Dr. Karen Kaufman
132 East 72nd St., NYC 10021
(212) 639–9614

Eva Lapidos
331 East 71st St., #1C, NYC 10021
(212) 864–7612

Rob Muller
2600 Netherland Ave., Bronx, NY
10463
(718) 884–2215

Laurie Oestreich
241 Central Park West, NYC 10024
(212) 721–8664

Dr. Sonia Orenstein
241 Central Park West, #1D, NYC
10024 (212) 595–4041

Kristin Perry
159 West 82nd St., Ste. 1B, NYC
10024
(212) 579–5505

Dr. Roger Rahtz
1349 Lexington Ave., NYC, 10128
(212) 369–2179

Phillip Reparsky
Bellevue Hospital Center
462 First Ave., Admin. Bldg. A259,
NYC 10016
(212) 562–8657

Dr. Laurence Saul
7 East 68th St., NYC 10021
(212) 327–0753

Melanie Schmich
344 West End Ave., NYC 10024
(212) 799–0900

Dr. Gary Schlesinger
27 West 72nd St., NYC 10023
(212) 877–7451

Dr. Michele Shackelford
*Lenox Hill Hospital Center for Attention
& Learning Disorders (CALD)*
1430 Second Ave., NYC 10021
(212) 434–4594

Dr. Sarita Singh
8 East 96th St., NYC 10128
(212) 828–5336

Allison Sitrin
573 10th St., Brooklyn, NY 11215
(917) 743–8204

Dr. Marjory Slobetz, CSC
556 16th St., Brooklyn, NY 11215
(718) 768–2900

Joan Swanson
140 West End Ave., Apt 1G, NYC
10023
(212) 769–2200

Michael Sweeney, Ph.D.
30 West 70th St., NYC 10023
(212) 362–2820

Barbara Thacher
26 Court St., Ste. 2700, Brooklyn, NY
11242
(718) 875–2890

Pia Wikstrom, Ph.D.
Manhattan Speech & Language
50 West 72nd St., NYC 10023
(212) 724–2580

MEDICAL PROFESSIONALS

Allergy

Dr. John Bent
Nose and Throat Specialist
186 East 72nd St., 2nd fl., NYC 10021
(212) 327–3000

Dr. Arthur DeLuca
269–01 76th Ave., New Hyde Park,
NY 11042
(718) 470–3585

Dr. Mary DiMaio
Pulmonologist
1440 York Ave., NYC 10021
(212) 988–5008

Dr. Arthur Lubitz
(not pediatric specialist)
30 East 40th St., NYC 10016
(212) 685–4765
450 7th Ave., NYC 10001
(212) 868–2802

Dr. David Mazza
7 Lexington Ave., Ste. 3, NYC 10010
(212) 677–7170

Dr. Ingrid Rosner
301 East 66th St., NYC 10021
(212) 650–9000

Dr. Rosalinda Rubenstein
1016 Fifth Ave., NYC 10028
(212) 737–2996

Dr. Hugh Sampson
5 East 98th St., 10th fl., NYC 10029
(212) 241–5548

Dr. A. Schneider
159 Clinton St., Brooklyn, NY 11201
(718) 624–6495

Dr. Morton Teich
930 Park Ave., NYC 10028
(212) 988–1821

Dr. Michael Teitel
35 East 35th St., NYC 10016
(212) 685–4225

Dr. David Wertheim
310 East Shore Rd., #308, Great Neck,
NY 11023
(516) 487–1073

Asthma

Dr. Arthur DeLuca
269–01 76th Ave., New Hyde Park,
NY 11042
(718) 470–3585

Dr. Allen Dozer
*Pediatric Pulmonology, NY Medical
College*
Munger Pavillion, Room 106,
Valhalla, NY 10595
(914) 493–7585

Dr. David Mazza
7 Lexington Ave., Ste. 3, NYC 10010
(212) 677–7170

Dr. Ingrid Rosner
301 East 66th St., NYC 10021
(212) 650–9000

Dr. Rosalinda Rubenstein
1016 5th Ave., NYC 10028
(212) 737–2996

Attention Deficit Hyperactivity Disorder

Dr. Marilyn Agin
79 Laight St., #1A, NYC 10013
(212) 274–9180

Dr. Paul Aronow
25 Canterbury Rd., Great Neck, NY
11021
(516) 466–9811

Dr. Vijaya Atluru
400 South Oyster Bay Rd., Hicksville,
NY 11801
107 Mineola Blvd., Mineola, NY
11501
1 Healthy Way, Oceanside, NY
11572
(516) 937–3508

Dr. Celia Blumenthal
1070 Park Ave., NYC 10128
(212) 534–7155

Dr. Ian Canino
28 West 71st St., NYC 10023
(212) 877–4180

Dr. John Garwood
Developmental Pediatrics
5 East 98th St., 8th fl., NYC
10029
(212) 241–4076; (212) 241–6710

Dr. Alyson Gutman
Schneider Children's Hospital, LIJ
1983 Marcus Ave., #130, Lake
Success, NY 11042
(516) 802–6130

Dr. Stanley Hertz
55 Fern Dr., Roslyn, NY 11576
(516) 484–6366

Dr. Glenn Hirsch
NYU/Eastbridge Child Study Center
577 First Ave., NYC 10016
(212) 263–8704

Dr. Ronald Jacobson
Pediatric Neurological Associates
125 South Broadway, White Plains,
NY 10605
(914) 997–1692

Dr. David Kaufman
3 East 83rd St., NYC 10028
(212) 737–4911

Dr. Steven Kurtz, Ph.D.
NYU/Eastbridge Child Study Center
577 First Ave., NYC 10016
(212) 263–8915

Dr. Barbara Lino, Ph.D.
166 West 88th St., NYC 10024
(212) 927–5359

Dr. Michael Merkin
30 West 13th St., NYC 10011
(212) 737–3054

Dr. Ruth Nass
New York University
400 East 34th St., NYC 10016
(212) 263–7753

Dr. Joseph Nieder
1556 Third Ave., Ste. 60A, NYC 10128
(212) 876–5406

Dr. Randall Ross
15 West 12th St., Ste. 1F, NYC 10011
(212) 352–3354

Dr. Laurence R. Saul
7 East 68th St., NYC 10021
(212) 327–0753

Dr. Romaine Schubert,
Neuroscience, NY Methodist Hospital
263 7th Ave., Ste. 5C, Brooklyn, NY
11215
(718) 246–8614

Dr. Michele Shackelford
*Lenox Hill Hospital Center for Attention
& Learning Disorders (CALD)*
1430 Second Ave., NYC 10021
(212) 434–4594

Dr. Sarita Singh
8 East 96th St., NYC 10128
(212) 828–5336

Audiology

Columbia Presbyterian Hospital
The Communications Center
186 East 76th St., 2nd fl., NYC 10021
(212) 327–3000

Dr. Michael Ditkoff
North Shore Otolaryngology Assoc.
333 East Shore Rd., Ste. 102,
Manhasset, NY 11030
(516) 482–8778

Jay Dolitsky
Dept. of Otolaryngology, NY Eye & Ear Infirmary
310 East 14th St., 6th fl., NYC 10003
(212) 979–4200

Dr. Donna Geffner
St. Johns University Speech & Hearing Center
8000 Utopia Pkwy., Queens, NY 11439
(718) 990–6480

Dr. Joseph Haddad
St. Johns University, Columbia University
161 Fort Washington Ave., NYC 10032
(212) 305–8933

Louise Levy
Cochlear Implant Center
210 East 64th St., NYC 10021
(212) 605–3793
863 Park Ave., Ste. 1E, NYC 10021
(212) 319–8423

Jane Madell
Beth Israel Medical Center, Phillips Ambulatory Care Center
10 Union Sq. East, Ste. 2K, NYC 10003
(212) 844–8792

Paul Mandele
The Listening Centre (Toronto-Tomatis)
599 Markham St., Toronto, Ontario
CANADA M6G2L7
(416) 588–4136

NY Eye and Ear Infirmary
310 East 14th St., NYC 10003
(212) 979–4000; (212) 979–4200;
(212) 979–4346

Dr. Robert Pincus
NY Otolaryngology Group
36A East 36th St., Ste. 200, NYC 10016
(212) 889–8575

Dr. Laurence Rosenblatt
103 South Beford Rd., Mt. Kisco, NY 10549
(914) 666–4290

St. Johns University Speech Hearing Center
8000 Utopia Pkwy., Queens, NY 11439
(718) 990–6480

Dr. Bill Shapiro
NYU Schwartz Health Care Center
530 First Ave., NYC 10006
(212) 263–7037

Speech Language Department
Beth Israel, Phillips Ambulatory Care Center
10 Union Sq. East, NYC 10003
(212) 844–8430

Autism/PDD

Dr. Mark Freilich
Total Kids Developmental
205 West End Ave., NYC 10023
(212) 787–2148

Dentistry

Dr. Mary George
173 East Shore Rd., Ste. 101 Great
Neck, NY 11023
(516) 487–8110 ·

Lois Jackson
505 LaGuardia Place, NYC 10012
(212) 995–8888

Dr. Michael King
30 East 40th St., Ste. 50, NYC 10016
(212) 986–2039

Dr. Gina Lodolini
241 Lexington Ave., Mt. Kisco, NY
10549
(914) 242–2000

Dermatology

Dr. Kathleen Davis
568 Broadway, Ste. 303, NYC 10012
(212) 334–1155

Endocrinology

Dr. Mariano Castro-Magana
120 Mineola Blvd., Mineola, NY 11501
(516) 663–3090

Dr. Madeleine Harbison
Weill Medical College
525 East 68th St., #M602, NYC
(212) 746–3462

Dr. Alfred Slonim
North Shore University Hospital
1165 Northern Blvd., Manhasset, NY
11030
(516) 869–3390; (516) 616–0074

Dr. Elizabeth Wallach
*Pediatric Endocrinology & Diabetes
Center*
5 East 98th St., NYC 10024
(212) 241–6936

Genetic Disorders

Jenna Antonelli
Schneider Children's Hospital
269-01 76th Ave., Rm. CH-009, New
Hyde Park, NY 11040
(718) 470–3010

Dr. Kwame Anyane-Yeboa
Columbia Presbyterian
6 North, Room 601A, 3959
Broadway, NYC 10032
(212) 305–6731

Dr. Joyce Fox
Schneider Children's Hospital
269-01 76th Ave., Rm CH-009, New
Hyde Park, NY 11040
(718) 470–3010

Dr. Judith Willner
*Dept. of Human Genetics, Mount Sinai
Hospital, Faculty Practice Associates,
Genetic Medicine*
1468 Madison Ave., NYC 10029
(212) 241–6947

Homeopathy

Dr. Anthony Aurigcmma
133 East 73rd St., NYC 10021
(212) 988–4800

Learning Disabilities

Dr. Steven M. Alter, Ph.D.
117 West 72nd St., Ste. 5E NYC
10023
(646) 872–6229
110–45 Queens Blvd., Ste. A2, Forest
Hills, NY 11375
(718) 261–3363

Dr. Elizabeth Auricchio
Educational Evaluator
5 East 78th St., NYC 10021
(212) 228–9350, (212) 879–9046

Colleen M. Berge, MA
255 Westfield Ave., Ste. 1A, NYC
10023
(212) 496–7029

Darcy Dean, CSW
230 West 13th St., NYC 10011
(212) 741–5182

Dr. William Dince
5 East 76th St., NYC 10021
(212) 535–7350

Dr. Martha Eddy
523 West 121st St., #43 NYC 10027
(212) 864–5188

Dr. Diana Feit, Ph.D.
201 East 87th St., NYC 10128
(212) 722–2639

Dr. Shoshana Goldman
Speech & Language Pathology
451 West End Ave., Apt 2E, NYC
10024
(212) 362–3071

Rita Haggerty, Ph.D.
1120 Park Ave., NYC 10128
(212) 289–6406

Dr. Arthur Heiserman
20 West 86th St., Ste. 1B, NYC
10024
(212) 362–5071

Karen Louick, MA, CCC
17 7th Ave., Brooklyn, NY 11217
(718) 638–0168

Janine Pollack
LAMM Institute
110 Amity St., Brooklyn, NY 11201
(718) 780–1668

Dr. David Salsberg
Rusk Institute
60 Madison Ave., #907, NYC 10010
(212) 263–6168

Michele Shackelford, Ph.D.
*Lenox Hill Hospital Center for Attention&
Learning Disorders (CALD)*
1430 Second Ave., NYC 10021
(212) 434–4594

**SUNY Optometric, The Optometric
Center of New York**
33 West 42nd St., NYC 10036
(212) 780–5060

Teachers College Center for Education
525 West 120th St., NYC 10027
(212) 678–3000

Dr. Donna Zanolla
2600 Netherland Ave., Ste. 108,
Riverdale, NY 10463
(212) 642–5849

Neurology

Dr. Vijaya Atluru
400 South Oyster Bay Rd., Hicksville,
NY 11801
107 Mineola Blvd., Mineola, NY
11501
1 Healthy Way, Oceanside, NY 11572
(516) 937–3508

Dr. Karen Ballaban-Gil
Children's Hospital at Montefiiore
1515 Blondell Ave., Bronx, NY 10461
(718) 405–8140

Dr. Gail Bedi
171 East 74th St., Ste. C2, NYC
10021
(212) 288–1001

Dr. Harvey Bennette
LAMM Institute
110 Amity St., Brooklyn, NY 11201
(718) 780–1668

Dr. Marcia Bergtraum
3003 New Hyde Park Rd. New Hyde
Park, NY 11040
(516) 488–2323

Dr. Regina DeCarlo
2550 Victory Blvd., 3rd fl., Staten
Island, NY 10314
(718) 983–0923

Dr. Orrin Devinsky
Epilepsy & Pediatric Neurology, NYU
Medical Center
403 East 34th St., 4th fl., NYC 10016
(212) 263–8871

Dr. Aleksandra Djukic
300 Community Dr., Manhasset, NY
11030
(718) 920–3450

Dr. Lydia Eviatar
269-01 76th Ave., New Hyde Park,
NY 11040
(718) 470–3453

Dr. Irving Fish
NYU Medical Center
550 First Ave., NYC 10016
(212) 263–6464

Dr. Muriel Frischer, Ph.D.
54 Montgomery Place, Brooklyn, NY
11215
(718) 857–8310

Dr. Alyson Gutman
Schneider Children's Hospital, LIJ
1983 Marcus Ave., #130, Lake
Success, NY 11042
(516) 802–6130

Dr. Syed Hosain
(for 24 video EEG)
NY Presbyterian Hospital
428 East 72nd St., Ste. 100, NYC
10021
(212) 746–3278

Dr. Ronald Jacobson
Pediatric Neurology
125 South Broadway, White Plains,
NY 10605
(914) 997–1692

Dr. David Kaufman
3 East 83rd St., NYC 10028
(212) 737–4911

Dr. Ranga Krishna
3262 Westchester Ave., Bronx, NY
10461
(718) 904–0908

Dr. Joseph Maytal
269-01 76th Avenue, New Hyde Park
NY 11040
(718) 470–3450

Dr. Ruth Nass,
New York University
400 East 34th St., NYC 10016
(212) 263–7753

Dr. Marc Patterson
Columbia Child Neurology Associates
180 Fort Washington Ave., NYC
10032
(212) 305–6038

Dr. Steven Pavlakis
1 Gustave L Levy Pl., NYC 10010
948 48th St., 3rd fl., Brooklyn, NY
11219
(718) 283–8669

Dr. Janine Pollack
LAMM Institute
110 Amity St., Brooklyn, NY 11201
(718) 780–1668

Dr. Jay Rosenblum
175 East 79th St., NYC 10021
(212) 249–7867

Dr. Ann Valentino
Neuropsychology
153 Waverly Place, NYC 10014
(212) 675–8591

Dr. Rueven Weiss
1099 Targee St., Staten Island, NY
10304
(718) 448–3210

Dr. John Wells
109 East 67th St., NYC 10021
(212) 772–6683

Dr. Agnes Whitaker
15 West 72nd St., Ste. 1P, NYC 10023
(212) 579–5557

Dr. Steven Wolf
*Dept. of Pediatric Neurology, Beth Israel
Medical Center*
10 Union Sq. East, Ste. 5J, NYC 10003
(212) 870–8506

Nutrition

Mary Beth Augustine, RD,CDN
*The Continuum Center for Health &
Healing*
245 5th Ave., 2nd fl., NYC 10016
(646) 935–2220

Great Plains Labs
GFCF Testing
11813 West 77th St., Lenexa, KS 66214
(913) 341–8949

Elyse Sosin
418 71st St., 1st fl., NYC 10021
(212) 327–2989

Ophthalmology

Dr. Ira Bernstein
Family Vision Care Associates
70 Westchester Ave., White Plains,
NY 10604
(914) 948–0304

Brian Campolattaro
30 East 40th St., NYC 10016
(212) 684–3980

Dr. Emily Ceisler
40 West 72nd St., NYC 10023
(212) 981–9800

Dr. Pamela Gallin
635 West 165th St., Ste. 224, NYC
10032
(212) 305–5407

Dr. Steven Kane
635 West 165th St., NYC 10032
(212) 927–8722

Dr. Sara Khun
60 Riverside Dr., NYC 10024
(212) 724–7201

Dr. Maury Marmor
146 Manetto Hill Rd., Plainview, NY
11803
(516) 942–4400

Dr. Hilary J. Ronner
136 East 64th St., NYC 10021
(212) 935–7272

SUNY Opthamology
Vision Training
33 West 42nd St., 5th fl., NYC 10036
(212) 780–4962

Dr. Mark Steele
40 West 72nd St., NYC 10023
(212) 981–9800

Dr. Jay Wisnicki
10 Union Sq. East, NYC 10003
(212) 844–2020

Optometry

Dr. Martin Lederman
10 Chester Ave., White Plains, NY
10601
(914) 684–6888

Dr. Fran Reinstein
77 Park Ave., Ste. 1G, NYC 10016
(212) 685–2457

Dr. Renee Richards
220 Madison Ave., NYC 10016
(212) 532–1168

Dr. Randy Schulman
139 Main St., Norwalk, CT 06851
(203) 840–1991

SUNY Optometric
33 West 42nd St., NYC 10036
(212) 780–4950

Dr. Andrea Thau
77 Park Ave., #1G, NYC 10016
(212) 685–2457

Dr. Joel Washowsky
33 West 42nd St., NYC 10036
(212) 780–4974

Orthopedics

Dr. Steven Burke
535 East 70th St., NYC 10021
(212) 606–1180

Dr. John Handelsman
Schneider Children's Hospital, LIJ
825 Northern Blvd., Great Neck, NY
11021
(516) 465–8660

Dr. Francisco LaPlaza
225 Community Dr., Great Neck, NY
11021
(516) 466–3131

Dr. Leon Root
535 East 70th St., Room 580, NYC
10021
(212) 606–1330

William Spielfogel
1 West 85th St., Ste. 1C, NYC
10024
(212) 874–0564

Dr. Richard Ulin
1095 Park Ave., NYC 10128
(212) 860–0905

Dr. Scott Zevon
75 Central Park West, NYC 10023
(212) 935–0686

Pediatrics

Dr. Marilyn Agin
Developmental Pediatrician
79 Laight St., #1A, NYC 10013
(212) 274–9180

Dr. Albert Aharon
410 Lakeville Rd., New Hyde Park,
NY 11042
(718) 831–1221

Dr. Dennis Allendorf
401 West 118th St., Ste. 2, NYC
10027
(212) 666–4610

Dr. Jane Aronson
151 East 62nd St., Ste. 1A, NYC
10021
(212) 207–6666

Dr. Ron Balamuth
393 West End Ave., NYC 10024
(212) 877–1118

Dr. Geeta Bhattacharya
200 Montague St., 2nd fl., Brooklyn,
NY 11201
(718) 422–8000

Dr. Harris Burstin
317 East 34th St., NYC 10016
(212) 362–3475; (212) 725–6300

Dr. Deniz Cereb
2315 Victory Blvd., Staten Island, NY
10314
(718) 982–9001

Dr. Lissiama Chaeko
18005 Hillside Ave., Jamaica, NY
11432
(718) 526–6300

Dr. Michelle Cohen
Tribeca Pediatrics
22 Harrison St., NYC 10013
(212) 226–7666

Dr. Seymour Cooper
173 Mineola Blvd., Ste. 100,
Mineola, NY 11501
(516) 746–2299

Dr. Jacqueline Cosme
390 West End Ave., Ste. 1E, NYC
10024
(212) 787–1444

Dr. Barbara Coven
Westchester Medical Group
210 Westchester Ave., 2nd fl., White
Plains, NY 10604
(914) 682–0731

Dr. Carmencita Diaz
21544 24th Ave., Bayside, NY
11360
(718) 428–7641

Dr. Lon Easton
Throgs Neck Pediatrics
3594 East Tremont, Bronx, NY
10465
(718) 863–1050

Dr. Genevieve Ferrier
West 11th St. Pediatrics
46 West 11th St., NYC 10011
(212) 529–4330

Dr. Mark Freilich
Total Kids Developmental
205 West End Ave., NYC 10023
(212) 787–2148

Dr. John Garwood
Developmental Pediatrics
5 East 98th St., 8th fl., NYC 10029
(212) 241–4076; (212) 241–6710

Dr. Adrian Gately
300 Park Pl., Brooklyn, NY 11238
(718) 622–0469

Dr. Carole Gervais
1886 Broadway, 2nd fl., NYC 10023
(212) 247–8100

Dr. Enriqueta Godoy
Long Island Medical Center
59–25 Kissena Blvd., Flushing, NY
11355
(718) 670–6100

Dr. Stanley Greenspan
4938 Hampden Lane, Ste. 229,
Bethesda, MD 20814
(301) 657–2348

Dr. Greg Gulbransen
229 South St., Oyster Bay, NY 11771
(516) 922–3131

Dr. Eric Gould
15 Barstow Rd., Great Neck, NY
11021
(516) 829–9409

Dr. Krishna K. Gupta
214-08 Hillside Ave., Queens Village,
NY 11427
(718) 217–0202

Dr. Carolyn B. Hiltebeitel
Westside Medical Associates
620 Columbus Ave., NYC 10024
(212) 877–1118

Dr. Diane Hochlerin
241 Central Park West, #1G, NYC
10024
(212) 787–1788

Dr. Eric Hollander
Mt. Sinai Hospital
1425 Madison Ave., Ste. 2266, NYC
10029
(212) 241–3623

Dr. Karen Hopkins
*NYU Medical Center, Developmental
Behavioral Pediatrics*
503 First Ave., Ste. 3A, NYC 10016
(212) 562–4313

Dr. David Horwitz
317 East 34th St., 3rd fl., NYC 10016
(212) 725–6300

Dr. Max Kahn
390 West End Ave., NYC 10024
(212) 787–1444

Dr. Lisa Kaufman
24 East 12th St., Ste. 403, NYC 10003
(212) 929–3313

Dr. Marie Keith
568 Broadway, Ste. 205 NYC 10012
(212) 334–3366

Dr. Kusum Khanna
235 West 75th St., NYC 10023
(212) 496–6440

Dr. Barbara Landreth
115 East 67th St., #1C, NYC 10021
(212) 772–7569

Lisanne Lange
2800 Marcus Ave., New Hyde Park,
NY 11042
(516) 622–7337

Dr. George Lazarus
3959 Broadway, NYC 10032
(212) 305–8585

Dr. Barbara Lino, Ph.D.
166 West 88th St., Ste. 2, NYC
10024
(212) 927–5359

Dr. Ronald London
Throgs Neck Pediatrics
3594 East Tremont Ave., Bronx, NY
10465
(718) 863–1050

Dr. Brian Lurie
3 School St., Ste. 302, Glen Cove, NY
11542
(516) 759–1234

Dr. Flavia Marino (bilingual)
155 East 38th St., #2E, NYC 10016
(212) 490–2446

Dr. Peter Masella
603 East 187th St., Bronx, NY 10458
(718) 733–3873

Dr. Cecilia McCarton
The McCarton Center
350 East 82nd St., NYC 10028
(212) 452–4264; (212) 996–9019

Dr. Clifford Mevs
Developmental Specialist
1534 Victory Blvd., Staten Island, NY
10314
(718) 980–5437

Dr. Ramon Murphy
Uptown Pediatrics
1245 East 96th St., NYC 10128
(212) 427–0540

Dr. Vicky Papadeas
505 LaGuardia Pl., #L3, NYC
10012
(212) 505–0222

Dr. Richard Perry
55 West 74th St., NYC 10023
(212) 595–0116

Dr. Janine Pollock
LAMM Institute
110 Amity St., Brooklyn, NY 11201
(718) 780–1668

Dr. Barry Price
263 7th Ave., Ste. 4H, Brooklyn, NY
11215
(718) 369–8170

Queens Pediatrics
158-49 84th St., Howard Beach, NY
11414
(718) 322-FINE

Drs. William & Irwin Rappaport
9 East 68th St., Ste. 1C, NYC
(212) 777–8407

Dr. Nonna Rivkin
108–48 70th Rd., Forest Hills, NY
11375
(718) 263–2072

Dr. Frank Roberto
1575 Hillside Ave., New Hyde Park,
NY 11040
(516) 488–1900

Dr. Lori Rosello
46 West 11th St., NYC 10011
(212) 529–4330

Dr. Michael Rosenbaum
West End Pediatrics
450 West End Ave., NYC 10024
(212) 769–3070

Dr. Suzanne Rosenfeld
West End Pediatrics
450 West End Ave., NYC 10024
(212) 769–3070

Dr. Asma J. Sadiq
10 Union Sq. East, NYC 10003
(212) 420–2000

Dr. Richard Saphir
55 East 87th St., #1G, NYC 10128
(212) 722–4950

Dr. Joseph Savitt
60–83 71st St., Maspeth, NY 11378
(718) 446–7562

Dr. Robin Schiff
2711 Henry Hudson Pkwy, Riverdale,
NY 10463
(718) 549–6229

Dr. Catherine R. Screnci
3 School St., Ste. 302, Glen Cove, NY
11542
(516) 487–1073; (516) 759–1234

Dr. Melissa Sedliss
Generalist
56 East 76th St., NYC 10021
(212) 249–5544

Dr. Jessica Sessions
110 West 97th St., NYC 10025
(212) 749–1820

Dr. Michele Shackelford
*Lenox Hill Hospital Center for Attention
& Learning Disorders (CALD)*
1430 Second Ave., NYC 10021
(212) 434–4594

Dr. Jacalyn Shafer
320 Central Park West, NYC 10025
(212) 579–4800

Dr. Joan Short
32 2nd St., Staten Island, NY
(718) 979–7472

Dr. Barry Stern
Carnegie Hill Pediatrics
1125A Park Ave., NYC 10128
(212) 289–1400

Dr. Marla Stern
55 East 87th St., #1G, NYC 10128
(212) 722–4950

Dr. Jennifer Trachtenberg
Carnegie Hill Pediatrics
1125A Park Ave., NYC 10128
(212) 289–1400

Dr. Max Van Guilder
241 Central Park West, NYC 10024
(212) 787–1788/89

Dr. Emilio Villegas
5917 Junction Blvd., Corona, NY
11368
(718) 334–6299

West End Pediatrics
450 West End Ave., NYC 10024
(212) 769–3070

Dr. Steven Wolf
10 Union Sq. East, NYC 10013
(212) 870–8506

Dr. Michael Yaker
West Side Pediatrics
620 Columbus Ave., #1, NYC 10024
(212) 874–4500

Dr. Sol Zimmerman
Pediatric Associates
317 East 34th St., 3rd fl., NYC 10016
(212) 725–6300

Psychiatry

Dr. Celia Blumenthal
1070 Park Ave., NYC 10128
(212) 534–7155

Dr. Roy Boorady
NYU Child Study Center
577 First Ave., NYC 10016
(212) 263–2771

Dr. Lynn Burkes
185 West End Ave., #1E, NYC
10023
(212) 362–5920

Dr. Karen Burkhard
994 West Jericho Tpke., Smithtown,
NY 11787
(631) 864–9200

Dr. Ian Canino
28 West 71st St., NYC 10023
(212) 877–4180

Dr. Michelle Ann Cervone
156 5th Ave., Ste. 823, NYC 10010
(646) 486–4287

Lee Cohen
623 Warburton Ave., Hastings-on-
Hudson, NY 10706
(914) 478 1330

Dr. Sarah Fox
210 West 89th St., #1D, NYC 10024
(212) 874–4558

Dr. Richard Gallagher
NYU Child Study Center
577 First Ave., NYC 10016
(212) 263–6622

Marianne Goldberger
907 5th Ave., NYC 10021
(212) 734–3400

Dr. Stanley Hertz
55 Fern Drive, Roslyn, NY 11576
(516) 484–6366

Dr. Michelle Hirsch
401 West End Ave., NYC 10024
(212) 724–8305

Dr. Marc Leonardo
303 East 83rd St., NYC 10028
(212) 452–0878

Dr. Owen Lewis
11 East 87th St., NYC 10128
(212) 996–8196

Dr. Alan Manevitz
60 Sutton Pl. South, Ste. 1CN, NYC
10022
(212) 751–5072

Dr. Anne McBride
525 East 68th St., NYC 10021
(212) 746–5720

Dr. Lois Mound
119 East 84th St., NYC 10028
(212) 744–0079

Dr. Jeffrey Newcorn
19 East 98th St., #5D, NYC 10029
(212) 659–8775

Dr. Richard Oberfield
200 East 33rd St., Ste. 2J, NYC 10016
(212) 684–0148

Dr. Melvin Otis
NYU Child Study Center
577 First Ave., NYC 10016
(212) 263–6622

Dr. Richard Perry
55 West 74th St., NYC 10023
(212) 595–0116

Dr. Ilene Rabinowitz
115 Central Park West, NYC 10023
(212) 579–5782

Dr. Cathy Raduns
10 East 90th St., Ste. 1A, NYC 10128
(212) 969–8860

Dr. Randall Ross
15 West 12th St., Ste. 1F, NYC 10011
(212) 352–3354

Dr. Laurence Saul
7 East 68th St., NYC 10021
(212) 327–0753

Dr. Ted Shapiro
525 East 68th St., NYC 10021
(212) 746–5713

Dr. Margaret Snow
55 East 72nd St., NYC 10021
(212) 861–4800

Dr. Robin Spirer
20 East 68th St., Ste. 203, NYC 10021
(212) 717–6502

Dr. Wendy Turchin
303 East 83rd St., NYC 10028
(212) 706–1957; (212) 706–1791

Dr. Alan Wachtel
201 East 87th St., NYC 10128
(212) 348–0175

Dr. Alex Weintrob
12 West 96th St., Ste. 1D, NYC
10025
(212) 662–9513

Mark Wilson
Columbia University
115 Central Park West, #5, NYC 10023
(917) 441–2344

Meg Wolder
(212) 434–3365

Psychology

Steven M. Alter, Ph.D.
117 West 72nd St., Ste. 5E, NYC
10023
(646) 872–6229
110–45 Queens Blvd., Ste. 2A, Forest
Hills, NY 11375
(718) 261–3363

Jeanne Angus, MA
25 West 95th St., NYC 10025
(646) 698–3041

Dr. Georgi Antar
31 Washington Sq. West, NYC
10011
(212) 982–3737

Dr. Elizabeth Aurrichio
5 East 78th St., NYC 10021
(212) 228–9350/(212) 879–9046

Dr. Ron Balamuth
393 West End Ave., NYC 10024
(212) 877–1118

Dr. Sheri Baron
185 Millwood Rd., Chappaqua, NY
10514
(914) 762–2058

Dr. Gail Bede
171 East 74th St., Ste. C2, NYC 10021
(212) 288–1001

Dr. Victoria Beech
3 East 68th St., NYC 10021
(212) 628–9200

Dr. Elizabeth Cooper-Camp
185 Court St., Brooklyn, NY 11201
(718) 858–5100

Dr. Clare Cosentino
15 West 12th St., NYC 10011
(212) 627–0078

Dr. William Dince, Ph.D.
5 East 76th St., NYC 10021
(212) 535–7350

Dr. Norma Doft
295 Central Park West, #4A, NYC
10024
(212) 787–5046

Dr. Ellen Farber
200 East 94th St., NYC 10128
(212) 987–5651

Dr. Diana Feit
201 East 87th St., NYC 10028
(212) 722–2639

Steven Friedfeld, CSW
231 East 7th St., Ste. 1K, NYC 10021
(212) 744–8737

Dr. Muriel Frischer, Ph.D.
54 Montgomery Pl., Brooklyn, NY
11215
(718) 857–8310

Shoshana Goldman
Speech-Language Pathology,
Psychotherapy
451 West End Ave., NYC 10024
(212) 362–3071

Sandy Greenbaum, CSW
Special Skills Groups, PreK-8th
27 West 72nd St., Ste. 319, NYC 10023
(212) 362-3475

Dr. Arthur Heiserman
20 West 86th St., Ste. 1B, NYC 10024
(212) 362-5071

Karen Kaufman, CSW
132 East 72nd St., NYC 10021
(212) 639-9614

Dr. Barbara Kenner, Ph.D.
Neuropsychological Assessment &
Consultation Services
5 East 76th St., NYC 10021
(212) 327-4979

Michelle Kornbleuth, Ph.D.
5 East 76th St., NYC 10021
(212) 327-4979

Dr. Eva Lapidos
331 East 71st St., #1C, NYC 10021
(212) 861-7612

Dr. Barbara Lino, Ph.D.
Psychoeducational Evaluations
161 West 88th St., Ste. 2, NYC 10024
(212) 927-5359

Dr. Antoinette Lynn
Educational Psychologist
350 Central Park West, Ste. 1Q, NYC
(212) 666-3180

Dr. Judith Moskowitz
Psychoeducational Evaluations
547 Saw Mill River Rd., Ardsley, NY
10502
(914) 674-0354

Dr. Andrew Morrel
140 West 79th St., NYC 10024
(212) 721-3710

Dr. Jeffrey Newcorn
Mt. Sinai Hospital
19 East 98th St., #5D, NYC 10029
(212) 659-8775

Barbara Novick, Ph.D.
999 5th Ave., NYC 10028
(212) 650-1021

Dr. Richard Oberfeld
200 East 33rd St., Ste. 2J, NYC 10016
(212) 684-0148

Laurie Oestreich, MSW
241 Central Park West, NYC 10024
(212) 721-8664

Dr. DeAnsin Parker
Goodson Parker Wellness Center,
Education, Development, Psychoanalysis
30 East 76th St., 4th fl., NYC 10021
(212) 717-5273; (212) 988-0898

Dr. Richard Perry
55 West 74th St., NYC 10023
(212) 595-0116

Dr. Janine Pollock
LAMM Institute
110 Amity St., Brooklyn, NY 11201
(718) 638-0168

Dr. Dale Ryan
666 West End Ave., Ste. 1A, NYC
10025
(212) 787-5812

Dr. David Salsberg
Pediatric Psychologist, Rusk Institute
60 Madison Ave., #907 NYC 10010
(212) 263-6168

Dr. Cory Scalzo, Ph.D.
Cognitive Assessment Services, Inc.
Bronxville, NY
(914) 793-2301

Dr. Gary Schlesinger
27 West 72nd St., NYC 10023
(212) 877-7451

Dr. Barry Schrem
Asst. Prof. Pediatrics, Albert Einstein
College of Medicine
125 Riverside Dr, Ste. 1C, NYC 10024
(212) 362-1509

Dr. Nancy Schultz
136 East 92nd St., NYC 10128
(212) 427–0119

Susan Schwartz, Ph.D.
1160 5th Ave., NYC 10029
(212) 426–0232

Gabrielle Shatan, Ph.D.
415 Central Park West, Ste. BL, NYC
10025
(212) 665–4898

Dr. Sarita Singh
8 East 96th St., NYC 10128
(212) 828–5336

Dr. Jonathon Sinowitz
370 Central Park West, NYC
10025
(212) 866–1171; (212) 665–4903

Buffy Smith
590 West End Ave., NYC 10024
(212) 787–2853

Dr. Margaret Snow
55 East 72nd St., NYC 10021
(212) 861–4800

Dr. Anne Steinberg
999 5th Ave., NYC 10028
(212) 472–7536

Dr. Barbara Thacher
26 Court St., Ste. 2700, Brooklyn, NY
11242
(718) 875–2890

Dr. Anne Valentino
153 Waverly Pl., NYC 10014
(212) 675–8591

Dr. Nancy Eppler Wolff
107 West 86th St., NYC 10024
(212) 595–5070; (212) 969–8860

Dr. Donna Zanolla
2600 Netherland Ave., Ste. 108,
Riverdale, NY 10463
(212) 642–5849

Psychopharmocology

Dr. Roy Boorady
NYU Child Study Center
577 First Ave., NYC 10016
(212) 263–2771

Topher Collier
*Park West Practice of Child, Adolescent &
Adult Psychiatry*
115 Central Park West, #5, NYC 10023
(212) 675–2254

Dr. Gianni Fredda
245 East 50th St., NYC 10022
(212) 644–3111

Dr. Eric Hollander
Mt. Sinai Hospital
1425 Madison Ave., Ste. 2266, NYC
10029
(212) 241–3623

Dr. Marc Leonardo
303 East 83rd St., NYC 10028
(212) 452–0878

Dr. Farhan Matin
1430 2nd Ave., Ste. 103, NYC 10021
(212) 434–4931

Dr. Anne McBride
525 East 68th St., NYC 10021
(212) 746–5720

Dr. Joseph Nieder
1556 Third Ave., Ste. 60A, NYC 10128
(212) 876–5406

Dr. Jeffrey Newcorn
Mt. Sinai Hospital
19 East 98th St., 5D, NYC 10029
(212) 659–8775

Dr. Melvin Oatis
NYU Child Study Center
577 First Ave., NYC 10016
(212) 263–6622

Dr. Mark Owens
110 Amity St., 3rd fl., Brooklyn, NY
11201
(718) 499–7733

Dr. Laurence Saul
7 East 68th St., NYC 10021
(212) 327–0753

Dr. Robyn Spirer
20 East 68th St., Ste. 203, NYC 10021
(212) 717–6502

Mark Wilson
Columbia University
115 Central Park West, #5 NYC
10023
(917) 441–2344

Traumatic Brain Injury

Dr. Jeffrey H. Wisoff
*Director, Division of Pediatric
Neurosurgery, New York University*
317 East 34th St., 10th fl., NYC
10016
(212) 263–6419

Urology

Dr. William Brock
Pediatric Urology Associates
1999 Marcus Ave., Ste. M18, Lake
Success, NY 11042
(516) 466–6953

RECOMMENDED WEB SITES

• About.com message boards
• www.aboutourkids.org
• www.allkindsofminds.org
• www.aspennj.org
• www.autismshop.com
• www.bigsplace.com
• www.braintalk.org (Web site at
  Massachusetts General Hospital)
• www.scilearn.com (Fast ForWord)
• www.grasp.org
• www.insideschools.com
• www.SchwabLearning.org
• www.speech-express.com

ADDITIONAL RESOURCES/ PARENT ADVOCACY CENTERS

Subscription to *Advanced Audiology,
Speech and Pathology* magazine
Advocates for Children, 151 West
30th St., NYC 10001, (212) 947–
3089
ADHD: The Great Misdiagnosis by Julian Stuart Harber, M.D
All Kinds of Minds, 24–32 Union Sq.
East, NYC 10003, (646) 775–6600
Bank Street Family Center
Behavior Modification Seminars led
by Dr. Barbara Wolf-Dorlester,
(212) 749–4457
Board of Education directory
Board of Education listing of special
education schools
The Center for Educational and Psychological Services (CEPS), Teachers College, Columbia University,
525 West 120th St., 6th fl., NYC
10027, (212) 678–3262
Children and Adults with Attention
Deficit Disorder (CHADD), 215
West 88th St., NYC 10024, (212)
721–0007
Children's Advisory Group, 155 West
72nd St., Ste. 201, NYC 10023,
(212) 769–4644
Churchill Center
Early Childhood Direction Center,
525 East 68th St., NYC 10021,
(212) 746–6175
Gateway School
GRASP, 135 East 15th St., NYC 10003
(646) 242–4003
Dr. Stanley Greenspan newsletter
and conferences
Dr. Madeleine Harbison (Cornell-
Weill Medical Center) for Prader-
Willi syndrome, 525 East 68th St.,
NYC 10021
Clara Hemphill, author of *New
York City's Best Public Elementary*

Schools: A Parents' Guide (Third Edition, 2003), *New York City's Best Public Middle Schools: A Parents' Guide* (Second Edition, 2004), and *New York City's Best Public High Schools* (Second Edition, 2003)

How to Talk So Kids Will Listen, and Listen So Kids Will Talk by Adele Faber and Elaine Mazlish (1999). New York: Avon

International Dyslexia Association

International Dyslexia Society

Jewish Board of Family and Children's Services, 120 West 57th St., NYC 10019 (212) 582–9100; 4049 Henry Hudson Pkwy, Bronx, NY 10471 (718) 796–8700

LAMM Institute, 110 Amity St., Brooklyn, NY 11201 (212) 780–1668

Learning Disabilities Association, 120 West 57th St., NYC

Legal Services for Children, 271 Madison Ave., Ste. 1007, NYC 10016, (212) 683–7999

Lindamood-Bell program (for audio issues), 26 East 64th St. NYC 10021, (212) 644–0650

Susan Luger, M.Ed and LCSW, Childrens Advisory Group, West 72nd St.

Manhattan Mothers subscription

National Alliance for Autism Research

National Center for Learning Disability, 381 Park Ave. South, Rm 1401, NYC 10016, (212) 684–5336

North East Westchester Special Recreation, Inc., 63 Bradhurst Ave., Hawthorne, NY 10532, (914) 347–4409

The OASIS Guide to Asperger's Syndrome: Advice, Support, Insight, and Inspiration, by Patricia R. Bashe, & Barbara L. Kirby (2001). New York: Crown.

Parentlink

Parents of A.N.G.E.L.S., 1968 Eastchester Ave., Bronx, New York 10461, (718) 931–0515

Parents League of New York, 115 East 82nd St., NYC 10028, (212) 737–7385

Parents in Action lectures by Mel Levine

Raising Cain: Protecting the Emotional Life of Boys by Dan Kindlon & Michael Thompson (2001). New York: Ballantine.

Raising Your Spirited Child: A Guide for Parents Whose Child Is More Intense, Sensitive, Perceptive, Persistant, Energetic by Mary Sheedy Kurcinka (1998). New York: HarperCollins

Reading for the Blind and Dyslexic for books on tape

Resources for Children with Special Needs, 116 East 16th St., 5th fl., NYC 10003, (212) 677–4650, Nina Lubin, Program Director

Resources for Children with Special Needs, *The Comprehensive Directory: Programs and Services for Children with Disabilities and Their Families in the Metro New York Area. www.resourcesnyc.org*

Siblings Without Rivalry: How to Help Your Children Live Together So You Can Live Too by Adele Faber, Elaine Mazlish (2002). Quill.

Sinergia, (212) 496–1300, using child advocate through this agency

Staten Island Mental Health Society

Tomatis Listening Program, The Spectrum Center, Contact Louise Levy

Understanding ADHD: The Definitive Guide to Attention Deficit Hyperactivity Disorder. by Christopher Green & Kit Chee (1998). New York: Ballantine.

Wrightslaw—several books related to Special Education Laws, authored by Peter W. D. Wright and others.

ATTORNEYS

Lauren Baum
1 Liberty Plaza, 23rd fl., NYC 10006
(212) 201–5426

Marion Katzive
317 Madison Ave., 21st fl., NYC 10017
(212) 500–5030

Michele Kule-Korgood
9820 Metropolitan Ave., # 2, Forest
Hills, NY 11375
(718) 261–0181

Mayerson and Associates
330 West 38th St., Ste. 600, NYC
10018
(212) 265–7200

NY Lawyers of the Public Interest
151 West 30th St., fl. 11, NYC 10001
(212) 244–4664

Amanda Oren
Mayerson and Associates
330 West 38th St., Ste. 600, NYC
10018
(212) 265–7200

Neal Rosenberg, Esq.
9 Murray St., NYC 10007
(212) 732–9450

Regina Skyer
276 Fifth Ave., NYC 10011
(212) 532–9736

Randy Waldman
151 West 30th St., NYC 10011
(212) 947–9779

AFTERSCHOOL PROGRAMS AND SUMMER CAMPS

Afterschool Programs

Aaron School Afterschool Program
309 East 45th St., NYC 10017
(212) 667–9594

ACT (Cathedral of St. John the Divine)
1047 Amsterdam Ave., NYC 10025
(212) 316–7540

Adler, Molly, Gurland, & Associates LLC
412 Avenue of the Americas, NYC
10013
(212) 477–4878; (212) 477–9838
124 East 84th St., NYC 10028
(212) 879–4688

All Star Fitness Center
Swim Lessons (weekends)
75 West End Ave., NYC 10023
(212) 265–8200

American Youth Dance Theater
434 East 75th St., NYC 10021
(212) 717–5419

Asphalt Green
1750 York Ave., NYC 10128
(212) 369–8890

Bailin-Mann Associates
603 East 23rd St., Brooklyn, NY
11210
(718) 859–3367

Ron Balamuth, Floor Time
393 West End Ave., NYC 10024
(212) 877–1118

Ballet Academy East
1651 Third Ave., 3rd fl., NYC 10128
(212) 410–9140

Bay Terrace YW/YMHA Project Child
212–00 23rd Ave., Bayside, NY
11360
(718) 423–6111

Brooklyn Friends
375 Pearl St., Brooklyn, NY 11201
(718) 852–1029

Brooklyn Heights Montessori
185 Court St., Brooklyn, NY 11201
(718) 858–5100

CATS
235 East 49th St., NYC 10017
(212) 751–4876

Chelsea Piers Gymnastics
23rd St. & Hudson River, NYC
10011
(212) 336–6666

Children's Aid Society
219 Sullivan St., NYC 10012
(212) 254–3074

Choice Time with Ms. Berman
PS 158
1458 York Ave., NYC 10021
(212) 744–6562

Churchill Afterschool Programs
301 East 29th St., NYC 10016
(212) 722–0610

Circus Gymnastics
2121 Broadway, NYC 10023
(212) 799–3755

Columbus Preschool and Gym
606 Columbus Ave., NYC 10024
(212) 721–0092

Corbin's Crusaders
321 West 78th St., Ste 6F, NYC 10024
(212) 875–8174

Dance at "The School at Steps"
2121 Broadway, NYC 10023
(212) 874–2410

Dance Theater Workshop
Ellen Robbins
219 West 19th St., NYC 10011
(212) 691–6500; (212) 924–0077

Discovery
251 West 100th St., NYC 10025
(212) 749–8717

Dome Project
486 Amsterdam Ave., NYC 10024
(212) 724–1780

Downtown Little School
15 Dutch St., NYC 10038
(212) 791–1300

Downtown Soccer League
295 Greenwich St., NYC 10007
(212) 274–1195

43rd Street Kids Preschool
484 West 43rd St., NYC 10036
(212) 564–7496

Friends Seminary Afterschool
222 East 16th St., NYC 10003
(212) 979–5030

Frozen Ropes
202 West 74th St., NYC 10023
(212) 362–0344

Future Kids Computer Camps
1628 First Ave., NYC 10028
(212) 717–0110

Gateway School
236 2nd Ave., NYC 10003
(212) 777–5966

Greenwich House Music School
Piano and Art Classes
46 Barrow St., NYC 10014
(212) 242–4770

**Guitar Lessons with
Kirk Huneycutt**
621 East 11th St., #3C, NYC
10009
(917) 674–3200

GymTime
1520 York Ave., NYC 10028
(212) 861–7732

**Hebrew School at Lincoln Square
Synagogue**
200 Amsterdam Ave., NYC 10023
(212) 874–6100

Integral Yoga
227 West 13th St., NYC 10011
(212) 929–0586

JCC in Manhattan
334 Amsterdam Ave., NYC 10023
(646) 505–4445

Jodi's Gym
244 East 84th St., NYC 10028
(212) 772-7633
25 Hubbles Dr., Mt Kisco 10514
(914) 244-8811

Juijitsu Concepts
79 Montgomery Ave., Scarsdale, NY 10583
(914) 723-7818

Kidfit
25 Dean St., Brooklyn, NY 11201
(718) 852-7670

Little Spirits
10 East 38th St., 3rd fl., NYC 10016
(212) 576-1018

Manhattan Tae Kwon Do East
1127 2nd Ave., NYC 10022
(212) 755-5982

Manhattan Samurai Sword
JCC in Manhattan
334 Amsterdam Ave., NYC 10023
(212) 505-4444

Marks Jewish Community House of Bensonhurst
7802 Bay Pkwy, Brooklyn, NY 11214
(718) 331-6800

Mohr's Explorer Program
640 Fort Washington Ave., #3D, NYC 10040
(212) 568-2820

The Music House
Private Lessons
111 Dyckman St., NYC 10040
(212) 569-4589

New York Conservatory of Music
Violin Lessons
321 East 69th St., NYC 10021
(212) 717-9590

New York Kids Club
Dance, Gym, & Karate Classes
265 West 87th St., NYC 10024
(212) 721-4400

Next Generation Yoga
200 West 72nd St., NYC 10023
(212) 595-9306

NOAR Program
92nd Street Y
1395 Lexington Ave., NYC 10001
(212) 415-5600

Oasis Children's Services
3 West 95th St., NYC 10025
(646) 698-1800

Pegasus Therapeutic Riding
Horseback Riding
204 Old Sleepy Hollow Rd.,
Pleasantville, NY 10570
Fox Hill Farm (office for above)
45 Church St., Ste. 205, Stamford, CT 06906
(203) 356-9504

PS 188 Afterschool Programs
Gym, Cooking
422 East Houston St., NYC 10002
(212) 677-5710

Robot Village
252 West 81st St., NYC 10024
(212) 799-7626

Rodeph Sholom Hebrew School
10 West 84th St., NYC 10024
(212) 362-8769

SCAN
307 East 116th St., NYC 10029
(212) 534-7800

Melanie Schmich
Play Therapy
344 West End Ave., NYC 10024
(212) 799-0900

Scope Dutch Broadway Elementary
1880 Dutch Broadway, Elmont, NY 11003
(516) 326-5550

Seido Karate
61 West 23rd St., NYC 10010
(212) 924-0511

74th Street Magic
510 East 74th St., NYC 10021
(212) 737–2989

Shaaray Tefila
Special Ed Hebrew School Class
250 East 79th St., NYC 10021
(212) 535–8008

Sol-Goldman Educational Alliance
344 East 14th St., NYC 10009
(212) 780–0800

Southeast Consortium for Special Services
740 West Boston Post Rd., Ste. 312, Mamaroneck, NY 10543
(914) 698–5232

Spirited Friends
250 Station Plaza, Ste. 33, Hartsdale, NY 10530
(914) 841–9847

Stephen Gaynor School
Mr. Rick's Athletics
22 West 74th St., NYC 10023
(212) 787–7070

Super Soccer Stars
145 West 88th St., NYC 10024
(212) 877–7171

Supermud Pottery
2744 Broadway, NYC 10025
(212) 865–9190

Sutton Gymnastics
636 Avenue of the Americas, NYC 10011
(212) 533–9390

Sylvan Learning Center
180 South Broadway, White Plains, NY 10605
(914) 948–4116

Take Me to the Water Swimming
120 East 89th St., NYC 10128
(212) 828–1756

3rd Street Music School Settlement
Piano
235 East 11th St., NYC 10003
(212) 777–3240

Throwback Sports
Mike Cohen, Team Sports & Coordination Skills
Upper West Side location
(212) 724–0630

Wee Dance Ballet
SOHO
(347) 661–9017

West End Day School
Chess Club & Rollerblading
255 West 71st St., NYC 10023
(212) 873–5708

West Side YMCA
Swimming lessons
5 West 63rd St., NYC 10023
(212) 875–4100

West Side Soccer League (WSSL) (weekends)
215 West 95th St., NYC 10025
(212) 479–7791

YM-YWHA of Washington Heights & Inwood
54 Nagle Ave., NYC 10040
(212) 569–6200

YM-YWHA of Riverdale
5625 Arlington Ave., Riverdale, NY 10471
(718) 548–8200

The Young People's Chorus of New York
150 East 87th St., NYC 10128
(212) 289–7779

Summer Programs

Adaptive Horseback Riding, Hidden Hollow Farm
84 Rte. 9N, Red Hook, NY 12571
(845) 758–0619

Adler, Molly, Gurland, & Associates LLC
412 Ave. of the Americas, NYC 10011
(212) 477–4878; (212) 477–9838
124 East 84th St., NYC 10028
(212) 879–4688

American Museum of Natural History
(weeklong programs)
Central Park West at 79th St., NYC
10024
(212) 769–5758

Asperger's Camp Grace Foundation
6581 Hylan Blvd., Staten Island, NY
10309
(718) 605–7500

Asphalt Green
555 East 90th St., NYC 10128
(212) 369–8890 ext.107

Bank Street Lower Camp
610 West 112th St., NYC 10025
(212) 875–4705

Bank Street Musical Theater Program
610 West 112th St., NYC 10025
(212) 875–4705

Baruch College Summer Camp
55 Lexington Ave., NYC 10010
(646) 312–5046/5040

Berkeley Carroll School Day Camp
181 Lincoln Place, Brooklyn, NY
11217
(718) 789–6060/638–1703

Boys Club of NY Department of Educational Services & Summer Programs
(212) 677–1108

Boy Scouts
www.scouter.com/compass/Where_To_Go/BSA_Camps

Buckley Country Day Camp
I.U. Willets Rd., Roslyn, NY 11576
(516) 365–7760

Camp at 92nd Street Y
1395 Lexington Ave., NYC 10128
(212) 415–5600

Camp Cayuga
Honesdale, PA
(908) 470–1224

Camp Chateaugay
Merrill, NY
(860) 350–8822

Camp Gorham
YMCA of Greater Rochester
265 Darts Lake Rd., Eagle Bay, NY
13331
(315) 357–6401; (888) 518–5671

Camp Half Moon
PO Box 188, Great Barrington, MA
01230
(413) 528–0940

Camp Hillard
Scarsdale, NY
(914) 949–8857

Camp Mohawk YMCA
PO Box 1209, Litchfield, CT 06759
(860) 672–6655

Camp Poyntelle
Summer
PO Box 66, Poyntelle, PA 18454
(570) 448–2161
Winter
212-00 Third Ave., Bayside, NY
11360
(718) 279–0690

Camp Southwoods
PO Box 459, White Plains, NY 10603
(914) 524–9200
NYS 532/Route 74 Paradox, NY
12858
(518) 532–7717

Camp Watonka
Hawley, PA
(570) 226–4779

Camp Winaukee
Center Harbor, NH
(603) 255–7272

Camp Yomi
K–4
1395 Lexington Ave., NYC 10128
(212) 415–5600

Central Park Early Learning
15 West 65th St., NYC 10001
(212) 787–5400

Chelsea Piers
23rd St. & Hudson River, NYC
10011
(212) 336–6846

Children's Aid
105 East 22nd St., NYC 10010
(212) 949–4800

Children's Museum of the Arts
(weeklong programs on art)
182 Lafayette St., NYC 10013
(212) 941–9198

Columbia Summer Camp
303 Lewisohn Hall, mailcode 4110,
2970 Broadway, NYC 10027
(212) 854–9699

Columbus Preschool and Gym
606 Columbus Avenue, NYC 10024
(212) 721–0090

Day Camp in the Park
(near Bear Mountain, NY)
6 Kendall Dr., New City, NY
10956
(845) 638–2515

Deerkill Day Camp
54 Wilder Rd., Suffern, NY 10901
(845) 354–1466

**Digital Video Boot Camp, Scarsdale
Middle School, & 3rd Eye Sports
Camp**
Scarsdale NY
(914) 722–1160

Discovery Program
251 West 100th St., NYC 10025
(212) 749–8717

Downtown Day Camp
Winter office:
55 Warren St., NYC 10007
(212) 766–1104, ext.224/229

Eagle Hill Academic
(half-day program)
45 Glenville Rd Greenwich, CT
06831
(203) 622–9240

East Hampton Indoor Tennis
(Hampton Country Day Camp)
PO Box 4149, 175 Daniels Hole Rd.,
East Hampton, NY 11937
(631) 537–8012

Eisner Camp
(reform Jewish sleepaway)
Brookside Rd., Great Barrington, NY
01230
(413) 528–1652
Winter address:
301 Route 17N Rutherford, NJ
07070
(201) 804–9700

**Fairfield Audubon Summer
Program**
2325 Burr St., Fairfield, CT 06824
(203) 259–6305

Fieldston Outdoors Ethical Culture
Fieldston School
Fieldston Rd., Bronx, NY
10471–3997
(718) 329–7352

Frozen Ropes Baseball Day Camp
202 West 74th St., NYC 10023
(212) 362–0344

Future Kids Computer Camp
1628 First Ave., NYC 10028
(212) 717–0110

Future Stars
546 Bedford Rd., Armonk, NY 10504
(914) 273–8500

Harbor Haven Day Camp
PO Box 1654 Livingston, NJ 07039
(973) 669–0800

Harlem RBI Baseball Activity Program
PO Box 871, Hell Gate Station, NYC 10029
(212) 722–1608

Interlocken International Camp
New Hampshire
(800) 862–7760

Iroquois Springs Sleepaway Camp
Winter
PO Box 20126, Dix Hills, NY 11746
(631) 462–2550
Summer
PO Box 487, Rock Hill, NY 12775
(845) 434–6500

Jamaica Bay Riding Academy
Equestrian Camp
7000 Shore Pkwy, Brooklyn, NY 11201
(718) 531–8949

Kew Forest Summer Camp
119–17 Union Tpke, Forest Hills, NY 11375
(718) 268–4667 ext.114

Landmark School Summer Program
429 Hale St., PO Box 227, Prides Crossing, MA 01965
(978) 236–3000

LearningSpring Elementary School
254 West 29th St., 4th fl., NYC 10001
(212) 239–4926

LuHi Summer Program
131 Brookville Rd., Brookville, NY 11545
(516) 626–1100

Magic Carpet Day Camp
61–35–220th St., Bayside, NY 11364
(718) 634–8109
Mailing address
PO Box 171, Fort Tilden, NY 11695

Marks Jewish Community Center House of Bensonhurst
7802 Bay Pkwy, Brooklyn, NY 11214
(718) 331–6800

Marymount
1026 Fifth Ave., NYC 10022
(212) 744–4486

Mount Tom Day Camp
48 Mount Tom Rd., New Rochelle, NY 10801
(914) 636–8130

Nature Place Day Camp
285 Hungry Hollow Rd., Chestnut Ridge, NY 10977
(845) 356–6477

New York Film Academy
100 East 17th St., 2nd fl., NYC 10003
(212) 674–4300

NYU Summer Program
Riverdale Country School
1981 Marcus Ave., Ste. 102, Lake Success, NY 11042
(212) 263–0760; (516) 358–1811

Ocean Beach Youth Group
PO Box 631, Ocean Beach, NY 11770
(631) 583–5300

Our Victory Day Camp
Dobbs Ferry, NY
(203) 329–3394; (800) 919–3394

Park Avenue Synagogue (with SEIT)
50 East 87th St., NYC 10128
(212) 369–2600

Pathfinder Country Day Camp
Summer
PO Box 807, Montauk, NY 11954
(631) 668–2080
Winter
PO Box 8631, Coral Springs, FL 33065
(800) 892–5532

Pegasus Therapeutic Riding
Horseback Riding
204 Old Sleepy Hollow Rd.,
Pleasantville, NY 10570
Fox Hill Farm (office for above)
45 Church St., Ste. 205, Stamford,
CT 06906
(203) 356–9504

Pierce Country Day Camp
Mineola Ave., Roslyn, NY 11576
(516) 621–2211

Poly Prep Country Day School Summer Programs
9216 7th Ave., Brooklyn, NY 11228–3698
(718) 836–9800 ext.322

Queens College Summer Program
65-30 Kissena Blvd., Flushing, NY 11376
(718) 997–2777

Ramah Day Camp
PO Box 807, Nyack, NY 10960
(845) 358–6240
3080 Broadway, NYC 10027
(212) 678–8884

Ramapo for Children
PO Box 266, Route 52, Salisbury
Tpke., Rhinebeck, NY 12572
(845) 876–8403

Ramapo Country Day Camp
600 Saddle River Rd., Airmont, NY 10952
(845) 356–6440

Resources for Children with Special Needs Summer Camps Directory
116 East 16th St., 5th fl., NYC 10003
(212) 677–4650

Riverbank State Park Summer Camp
679 Riverside Dr., NYC 10031
(212) 694–3600

Rutgers Presbyterian Church
236 West 23rd at Broadway, NYC 10023
(212) 877–8227 ext.212

St. Barts Day Camp
109 East 50th St., NYC 10022
(212) 378–0203

Seewackamano Camp
507 Broadway, Kingston, NY 12401
Summer
(845) 657–8288
Winter
(845) 338–3810

SportTime in the Hamptons
(631) 653–6767

SUNY College at Old Westbury
Route 107, Old Westbury, NY 11568
(516) 876–3490

Sunny Days Camp
Nightingale Bamford School
20 East 92nd St., NYC 10128
(212) 289–5020

Trailblazers 92nd St. Y
Grades 7–9
(212) 415–5600

Usdan Center for the Performing Arts Day Camp
NYC Office
420 East 79th St., NYC 10021
(212) 772–6060
LI Office
185 Colonial Springs Rd., Wheatley
Heights, NY 11798
(631) 643–7900

Vanderbilt YMCA
224 East 47th St., NYC 10017
(212) 756–9600 ext.640

Sample Referral Letter

Date
Chairperson
District _____
New York City Department of Education

To Chairperson,

I am writing on behalf of my child, _____, who is presently attending _____. I would like to have my child assessed in consideration for his/her eligibility to receive special education services in our school district. I understand that the initial assessment begins with an individual evaluation of my child. I would be grateful if you could provide me with a date as soon as possible, as I am aware that the process can take some time.

I understand that in order to receive special education services a child must receive an individualized educational program (IEP). I would like to request any information you can send me regarding this procedure, specifically what the steps are in order to determine a child's eligibility.

Thank you in advance for your assistance. I can be reached at the address and telephone number below.

I look forward to hearing from you.

Your Name
Address
Telephone (cell & home)
E-mail

Recommended Checklist for School Visits

❑ Speak to the school director, teacher, and therapists regarding schools for your child.

❑ Call schools to schedule tours—ask if you can get an application before the tour.

❑ Find out what type of evaluation each school requires and what other information they want for the application packet on your child.

❑ Evaluations: Do you have a current psychoeducational or neuro-psychological evaluation for your child? If not, you will need to schedule one *immediately*, as many schools require the evaluation as part of your packet and won't schedule an interview until the packet is complete. Points:
  • Talk to the evaluator about what the testing is for.
  • Have someone read the final written report; does it reflect who your child is?
  • Talk about the results related to any change in your child's classification.

❑ Attend school tours—be prompt; turn your cell phones off; speak to the person who gives the tour so they can put a face with your child's application (thanks, you really loved the school, etc.).

❑ Obtain applications.

❑ Complete applications—include a picture of your child; have someone read at least one of these to give you feedback on your responses.

❑ Send handwritten notes to schools (admissions director or staff member who gave the tour).

❑ If you have outside therapists, ask if they would be willing to write or call on your child's behalf. *Don't* have more than two people call, as it becomes annoying!

❑ Do you have any other contacts? Other parents whose children attend the school or someone who works at the school—people who could speak about your contribution to the school (fundraising, parent involvement, etc.)?

Schools Listed By Classifications

Autism (including Asperger's Syndrome and PDD)

Association for Metroarea Autistic Children, Inc. (AMAC)
Brooklyn Blue Feather Elementary (AHRC)
The Child School
The Hallen School
LearningSpring Elementary School
The League School
The McCarton School
Pathways School
Quality Services for the Autism Community Day School (QSAC)
The School for Language and Communication Development
(SLCD)

Blind

The Lavelle School for the Blind and Visually Impaired

Deaf

The Clarke NYC Auditory/Oral Center
New York School for the Deaf
The School for Language and Communication Development
(SLCD) —accepts hearing impaired secondary to a language
disorder

Emotionally Disturbed (ED)

Association for Metroarea Autistic Children, Inc. (AMAC)
Brooklyn Blue Feather Elementary (AHRC)
The Child School (only Asperger's Syndrome)
The Gillen Brewer School
The Hallen School
LearningSpring Elementary School
The League School (only Asperger's Syndrome)
The Lorge School
The Lowell School

The Martin De Porres School
The Reece School
The School for Language and Communication Development
    (SLCD)
The Summit School
West End Day School

Learning Disabled (LD)

The Aaron School
The Child School
The Churchill School
The Community School
Eagle Hill School
The Gateway School
The Gillen Brewer School
The Hallen School
LearningSpring Elementary School
The Lorge School
The Lowell School
The Mary McDowell Center for Learning
The Parkside School
The Reece School
The School for Language and Communication Development
    (SLCD)
The Stephen Gaynor School
The Summit School
West End Day School
Windward School
Winston Prep School
Yeshiva Education for Special Students (YESS!)

Mentally Retarded (MR)

Hebrew Academy for Special Children (HASC)
New York Foundling Center/John E. Coleman School
The School for Language and Communication Development
    (SLCD)

Multiple Disabilities (MD)

Brooklyn Blue Feather Elementary (AHRC)
Hebrew Academy for Special Children (HASC)

The Lavelle School for the Blind and Visually Impaired
New York Foundling Center/John E. Coleman School
The School for Language and Communication Development
  (SLCD)

Other Health Impaired (OHI)

The Aaron School
Brooklyn Blue Feather Elementary (AHRC)
The Community School (only ADD/ADHD)
The Gateway School
The Gillen Brewer School
The Hallen School
Hebrew Academy for Special Children (HASC)
LearningSpring Elementary School
The Lowell School
New York Foundling Center/John E. Coleman School
The School for Language and Communication Development
  (SLCD)
West End Day School
Yeshiva Education for Special Students (YESS!)

Speech Impaired (SI)

The Aaron School
Association for Metroarea Autistic Children, Inc. (AMAC)
The Child School
The Churchill School
The Community School
The Gateway School
The Gillen Brewer School
The Hallen School
LearningSpring Elementary School
The Lowell School
The Parkside School
The Reece School
The School for Language and Communication Development
  (SLCD)
Winston Prep School
West End Day School
Yeshiva Education for Special Students (YESS!)

Checklist for Applications

School: _____

Deadline for the application: _____

Date you sent the application (attach receipt): _____

Date reports from teachers/therapists sent: _____

Date school contacted regarding receipt of application: _____

Person you spoke to: _____

❑ Cover letter
❑ Application, including release form
❑ Current evaluations
❑ Current classroom report
❑ Current therapy/related services reports
❑ Current IEP
❑ Reports from other outside professionals
❑ Photo of your child
❑ Other possible documents—developmental history, tuition/financial aid forms, etc.
❑ Application fee

Glossary

ABA: Applied Behavior Analysis

ADD/ADHD: Attention Deficit Disorder or Attention Deficit/Hyperactive Disorder, which are identified under the classification of Other Health Impaired (OHI)

AS: Asperger's Syndrome

AUT: Autism

CBST: Central-Based Support Team, the New York State agency that gives final approval of a child's IEP, including special education services and placement in a public or private school

CO: Counseling, a related service identified on a child's IEP

CPSE: Committee on Preschool Special Education, which is the team of professionals in the Department of Education who are responsible for determining whether a child is eligible for special education services between the ages of 3 and 5 years

CSE: Committee on Special Education, which is the team of professionals in the Department of Education who are responsible for determining whether a student is eligible for special education services between the ages of 5 and 21 years

DSM–IV–TR: Diagnostic and Statistical Manual of Mental Disorders (4th Edition, Text Revision), which is published by the American Psychiatric Association and is used by professionals in the field of mental health to diagnose and treat children (and adults) based on specific diagnostic criteria

ED: Emotionally Disturbed

HI: Hearing Impaired

IEP: Individualized Education Program, which is created for a child who has been diagnosed with a disability by the Committee on Special Education

LD: Learning Disabled

MD: Multiple Disabilities

MR: Mentally Retarded

NPS: Nonpublic School, a listing of schools that have been approved by the New York State Education Department to provide placements for students who are classified as disabled, who are approved for funding for tuition, and for whom the New York City Department of Education does not have an appropriate school placement

NYCDOE: New York City Department of Education

NYSED: New York State Education Department

OHI: Other Health Impaired

OT: Occupational Therapy, a related service identified on a child's IEP

PDD: Pervasive Developmental Disorder, a diagnosis found in the *DSM–IV–TR*

PT: Physical Therapy, a related service identified on a child's IEP

SI: Speech Impaired

SL: Speech Therapy, a related service identified on a child's IEP

TBI: Traumatic Brain Injured

VI: Visually Impaired, including Blind

WISC–IV: *Wechsler Intelligence Scale for Children* (Fourth Edition, 2003)

WPPSI–R: *Wechsler Preschool and Primary Scale of Intelligence* (Revised Edition, 2002)

Index

About the Authors

Laurie DuBos, Ph.D., has been in the field of special education for over 30 years, with 15 years of classroom experience in private and public schools. She is a co-founder of the Gillen Brewer School, where she was the Director of the school-age program. She is currently an Assistant Professor in the Graduate School at the College of New Rochelle. Throughout her teaching and administrative experience, Dr. DuBos has worked with parents and their children who have been diagnosed with learning disabilities, behavioral and emotional disorders, speech and language delays, sensory disorders, PDD/Autism, and medical and other health impairments.

Jana Fromer is a graphic designer. She is a mother who has been involved in the world of special education for the past 8 years. Her personal experience within this wonderful community of families, children, and educators provided the inspiration to write this book.